Call of the Sea

France and Christian Guillain

Call of the Sea

Translated from the French by Caroline Hillier

HARPER & ROW, PUBLISHERS

New York, Hagerstown, San Francisco, London

This work was first published in France under the title *Le bonheur sur la mer.* © Editions Robert Laffont, S.A. 1974.

Grateful acknowledgment is made to Alfred A. Knopf, Inc., for permission to reprint the excerpts from *The Prophet* by Kahlil Gibran. Copyright 1923 by Kahlil Gibran; renewal copyright 1951 by Administrators C.T.A. of Kahlil Gibran Estate, and Mary G. Gibran.

The photographs are from the collection of France and Christian Guillain unless otherwise indicated.

FIRST U.S. EDITION

Designed by Dorothy Schmiderer

Library of Congress Cataloging in Publication Data

Guillain, France.
  Call of the sea.

  Translation of Le bonheur sur la mer.
  1. Voyages and travels—1951– 2. Seafaring
life. 3. Guillain, France. 4. Guillain, Christian. I. Guillain, Christian, joint author.
II. Title.
G530.G8913 1976   910'.41   75–23884
ISBN 0–06–011631–5

76 77 78 79 10 9 8 7 6 5 4 3 2 1

Contents

Color plates appear after page 58

A section of black-and-white photographs follows page 122

1

A Small Baby-a Small Boat

Three o'clock in the afternoon; our baby daughter Laurence, is asleep, and for a while I can do as I like, think my own thoughts. Sailing free, under mainsail alone, the *Alpha* slips gently along at three or four knots toward the southeast, toward the Canaries. We left Casablanca a week ago. The weather is what my aunt would call "ladylike": bright sun, a gentle wind, and a pleasantly calm sea. The perfect weather for getting a golden tan if it were hotter, but it is only the beginning of December. A ray of winter sunlight slants obliquely across the cabin, is reflected brilliantly from the metal of stove and sink.

A gentle torpor lulls us to sleep. A vague somnolence weighs us down, slows our reflexes. My mind floats effortlessly from my body, as if the rest of myself were dead. The weight of my body no longer inhibits me; I can focus my thoughts on whatever I like —our first seven days at sea—everything else.

I feel as if I have at last emerged from a long nightmare of numbness and exhaustion. I have adapted to my new situation: I am here on a small boat, at sea, with a baby a few weeks old.

And God knows we put up with enough criticism before setting out on this trial voyage.

"A baby on a boat! Madness!"

"It's absurd; leave her with us."

"Such a small boat, it's irresponsible of you . . ."

These reactions were understandable, of course. It would probably have been more "responsible" to have set ourselves up with our baby in Paris, in a small apartment. We could both work. Laurence would have a "real" bottle, in a "real" crib. She would go along real streets, into the real subway, have a generous share of dirt, breathe in her proper ration of exhaust fumes. She would have all the excitements of city life, and on Sundays we would take her to the park. A good doctor would see that she got rid of her colds and flu, and that she got enough vitamins. In fact, we would do our duty like everyone else.

On the *Alpha,* Laurence would only be breast fed, and her cradle would be perpetually rocked, so that she would have to adjust her balance even when she was asleep. Her body and clothes would be washed only in salt water. She would be in a violent, continual draft, night and day. Take care she doesn't get tonsilitis, bronchitis, all the other itises. She would inhale only iodine and salt.

"And what about storms! What will you do if there's a storm?"

"Don't worry; we won't make a point of putting her up on deck."

We had thought about our plan for nearly three years. We weren't setting out to sail around the world for the fun of it, or as an athletic feat. We were starting our family life on a boat. Before Laurence was born we had sailed on other people's boats. It was to live with Laurence that we built our "nest," in steel, a solid and perfectly watertight nest, our *Alpha.*

We hoped that one day we would have a large enough sailing boat to hold a lot of children. We would live close to nature, teach

2

them to read and write and do arithmetic, to play music, to sing, to laugh, to love life.

To love life. Since Christian and I met in Tahiti, in April, 1965, this is what has guided us and given us strength. Now, December 7, 1967, the *Alpha* is carrying us toward the Canaries; before this there were days and weeks and months of vicissitudes, during which we both have known much happiness and much unhappiness. We had to fight hard to build our family nest, our little home, which is so tiny compared with the vast Atlantic but so important to us. As I know well, have learned to my cost, nothing is given away free in life. My childhood, my youth, Christian's childhood and youth —very different paths which might never have crossed, and yet . . . If I set down in black and white everything that has made us, it is as if I were writing a novel expressly to show how two people meet at twenty, work through their neuroses together, and fight doggedly to define and shape the kind of life they want.

Laurence is asleep, cradled by the *Alpha.* As a family, we share together the warmth of the islands, the white sand, the palm trees that lean over the transparent waters of a lagoon teeming with fish. We love hunting, gathering fruit, the water, the pure air. We are friends, utterly and completely. The love between our bodies expresses our love of life, of our naked bodies in the sun, in the water, or on the sand, the love of all that is good together, of everything unique, of all that is productive; it was because of this that Laurence was born.

We have been at sea a week and Christian is already on his fourth novel: I have never seen him absorb so much literature. It's a pleasant way to keep one's mind alert. His only relaxation. Because except for the navigation he does everything single-handed. He glances regularly at the compass fixed at the head of his berth to check our course. Around him the sextant, the direction-finder, charts, and books on navigation remind me of his mission: he is responsible for the survival of the boat, of his wife and child.

My mission is different. And a baby takes up more time at sea than elsewhere. It isn't that I dislike the seaman's life. But from six in the morning till six at night I feed, change, and wash with scarcely a break, only stopping to prepare our meals. At sea, movements are slower, more tiring; the boat makes you use your muscles all the time. I feel perpetually overwhelmed by all there is to do.

Also, the *Alpha* was designed to be sailed by one person because I have to be absolutely free for Laurence, whatever happens. Christian didn't want to force the hard work of a seaman on me either, since being a mother at sea is difficult enough in itself. However, that doesn't stop me from time to time heaving on ropes so that my hands are rubbed raw, helping to hoist two anchors without a windlass, or diving to fish something out of the water.

Christian wanted a very strong hull and rigging that would stand up to anything. We didn't have much money, and the *Alpha* cost us a lot of elbow grease, imagination, and economizing— exhausting when one is expecting, and then feeding, a baby. Christian went from harbor to harbor in search of second-hand gear, finding a twenty-year-old sextant here, an airplane compass there. Winches, which were too expensive, were replaced by blocks and tackle, which help us, for instance, to hoist the jib. And the *Alpha,* with her very simple, but very solid, rigging and masts, now carries her precious cargo, our little family, toward Las Palmas in the Canaries.

I think back a week to our first day on the *Alpha* with Laurence. Sailing peacefully along, taking our time, with our whole lives in front of us. Outside, the sun was shining softly, and Laurence's pink bath thermometer registered sixty degrees. A light following wind drove us forward: seventy miles a day. We are sailing down to the Tropics, to the heat. Each day we gain one or two degrees. We are still wearing woolen clothes. Soon we'll be naked.

We're alone—Christian, Laurence, and I. But we have an excellent helmsman, the ideal crewman, who doesn't talk or eat, drink or smoke, who never complains and never sleeps: our automatic pilot. As it has a wind vane—a *girouette*—on top, we've christened it Gigi. Gigi was born in a workshop in Casablanca, where Christian cleverly knocked her together from a few bits of wood and metal, to a very precise plan. She keeps us on course better than any person could, at any speed. With a little flick of her tail she rights the boat in a masterful manner whenever a wave threatens to bring her round. She has complete control of the *Alpha.* We only have to take the tiller in very bad weather. She's fragile and we frequently say a prayer for her. If only she lasts as far as Las Palmas. Because if Gigi fails us—as I am completely monopolized by Laurence—Christian is the only man left at the helm. But we trust her. Happy to be on our *Alpha,* our new boat, we sail with a fair wind till evening.

The sea is very animated. Is this a good omen? It's certainly how I like it best. Just lively enough to bear the *Alpha* along in its dance, and giving us the long swell typical of these coasts. This fills me with energy, and I can wash the diapers as quickly as Laurence dirties them. The skipper looks askance at the guard rails with their decoration of white squares. "If I go about," he says, "the jibsheet and mainsheet will tear down everything on the port side." Nothing must get in the way. He's right. So the disputed articles will be confined to the stern rail, only seven and a half feet long. In view of the daily consumption of a small baby it's not very big. I will be forever fetching and carrying.

And suddenly I feel frustrated in my role as a woman. Nothing on board has been planned or thought out with me in mind. All too often on boats there is room only for men. However much yachting has developed, few women sailors go around the world. During the voyage they usually lead a man's life, and are very proud of being just as good sailors. In the West Indies I met a very solid German girl who was sailing alone from Hamburg to the Antilles and back. She was an irresistible force: she could easily do without windlass and winches on her thirty-three-foot sloop.

I have never seen a book relating the experiences of a wife and mother aboard a small sailing boat with a baby a few weeks old, yet I have met more than one family at sea. A woman armed with baby, makeup box, and women's magazines coming on board is like an ugly duckling appearing in the nest. She must make haste to become a swan. And time seems to drag when one is trying to get rid of the hateful gray down, when one feels ill at ease, disoriented. One hears oneself saying that the place of a "real" woman is not on a boat. I love sailing, the sea, the wind, the solitude, the sun, the natural and healthy life. A boat gives me all that. Yet, although it seems completely logical to me that the captain should be the only master on board, apart from God, for the sake of our safety and happiness, I still rebel against the permanent supervision of every-thing I do. It reminds me too much of my family. I lose my initia-tive, all my imagination and spontaneity.

As it is clear that without the *Alpha* we would be dead, the skipper decides the place for each object according to its impor-tance for the proper functioning of the boat. For example, it has been decided that the most practical place for the tools so that they are easily accessible is the cutlery drawer. When I want a knife, I have to move several pounds of metal. The oil left on a wrench often drips onto the spoons. Sometimes it makes me wild.

That first night on board, after our meal of rice and corned beef came the dishwashing. Armed with a five-gallon bucket, se-curely fixed to a rope, I drew up some sea water. If properly thrown, the bucket fills up immediately, giving my arm a hefty jolt, jerking me forward. I hold on tight to the rigging.

"I think we'll get a good night," says Christian. "It's a shame I haven't got a boom to hold the jib. With the wind taken out of it by the mainsail it's flapping and getting very worn. I'm going to lower it. . . . There are also Gigi's bolts to check."

At last everything is in order. The skipper has made his first night round on deck; the baby is sleeping well wrapped up. I stretch out and say "Good night."

It's completely dark in the cabin. Outside, the faint light of the stars barely mottles the sail. There's a new moon. Gradually the wind drops, then dies away completely. But the feebler it gets the more the *Alpha* rolls. The famous long swell is getting up. A long nightmare is beginning.

Without wind the boat goes mad. She rolls like a poor wretch who has lost her sense of balance. Her "wings" flap, quivering, useless. The boom swings stupidly from one side to the other, making the shackle on the mainsheet crack loudly each time on the steel hull. There is no breathing rhythm to adopt to feel more comfortable, because there's no rhythm. We're tossed in all direc-tions, furiously and rudely buffeted, with the added misery of knowing that we're making no progress. The ceaseless, irregular movement finally exhausts us. We go to sleep, but it's a vicious circle. We fall asleep, but at the same moment the sea jolts us and wakes us up. She'll make us pay for our dreams.

6

Christian goes up on deck at least ten times, but there's nothing he can do, except start the engine and take the tiller, which would only add to our misfortunes. Better to reconcile ourselves to the situation, save our pains and wait. As I'm breast feeding Laurence I can't risk being seasick. I take some Marzine, which knocks me out even more. Then, miraculously, I fall asleep.

The sun shines down on the minute *Alpha,* bravely breasting the waves. The cabin is now a nauseating gaping hole, where I have to make every effort not to be sick. But Laurence wakes up very bright and refreshed.

Our one dish is stewing in the Seb, our precious pressure cooker, securely fixed to the stove that Camping Gaz has given us. We have no gimbals, a system that would allow the Domino—the little stove—to keep in a horizontal position whatever the angle of the boat. Only a hermetically sealed pan can cope with the endless, sudden lists. For the same reason, for water we have a whistling kettle that is completely sealed. I guard the kettle and pan jealously, because they can't be replaced before the next port: no shops at sea. Each object becomes immensely precious. You don't waste anything, throw anything away. If the boat is disabled, a crossing planned for ten days can easily last a month, or more. So you have to provide for this and economize on water and food with it in mind.

Disaster: Just now, when I was emptying the dishwater, I threw out a teaspoon. We've only got two spoons left. That's why I hate the half-numbed state I'm in. I have no strength, my reflexes are slow, and I'm very clumsy. I grow more and more afraid of falling overboard each time I have to go on deck.

From the very first day Laurence was quite at home. For a start she sleeps seven hours at a stretch. This suits me, but I'm frequently tempted to wake her up to feed her. I wait patiently, and at last she opens one eye. Her little mouth works energetically at her wrists: soon there'll be the urgent cries of a hungry baby. I struggle against the sleep drugging me, and lay her down by my side. I mustn't go to sleep; I might smother her by rolling on her. Wedged against the bunk board, my back arced against the wood, I brace myself each time the boat rolls, to protect my baby.

Laurence continues at this slower pace for the first two days at sea, but she takes in a double amount at each meal. Then she returns to her usual four-hourly rhythm, but still with a ravenous appetite. After the first feeding I'm a bit worried. I tell myself a baby that age can't be seasick, but I can't prevent myself from watching over her anxiously for the next couple of hours: a baby only takes an hour and a half to digest its mother's milk—three hours for cow's milk. But it's all right. Her stomach is in better shape than ours.

Then I have to change and wash her. I sit on my bunk and hold Laurence in her basket between my feet, so that she can't roll either way. I give her a quick clean-up with cotton and baby oil, under a blanket because it's still cold. From time to time I warm her up with my breath.

Finally—the diapers have to be washed, the cute little squares and triangles I would gladly throw in a washing machine—or overboard. When you're broke and want a boat, disposable diapers are out of the question: we live on a hundred francs ($80) a month, which would just about cover their cost.

I quickly discovered that sea water is the best detergent. No need for soap, even for special salt-water soap. I lean over the side, plunge the things straight into the sea, and the sun takes care of disinfecting and bleaching them. Drying is another matter. With the wind behind us—our usual mode of sailing—a boat rolls a lot, and I have to hang on all the time. Because of the *Alpha's* small size a clothesline is impossible. I can hang only four diapers at a time on the sternrail. And one's always at the mercy of a clumsy wave that can break on the hull and wet the washing. You have to take all the things in at midday, when the sun is at its height, for otherwise they'll never dry. Whatever you do, the salt stays in and gradually everything grows damp.

After using one diaper, Laurence's skin was covered with little red spots. I was very upset. We couldn't possibly carry enough fresh water for the washing. What could I do? I found some thick white cream in the medicine box, which stuck obstinately to clothes and smelled strongly of cod-liver oil. I spread it on thick. A few hours later her skin was as good as new, completely. I continued to apply a thin layer until she got used to the salt. After four days I only needed to use talc. We'd won.

Years before Laurence was born, I had pored over books on

8

child care and child psychology. But life at sea upsets everything: it's the opposite of "normal." A regular life? You're always at the mercy of the weather or a technical hitch: a ripped sail, a parted rope. Then too, as we're sailing westward we're continually changing time. So from the start I never imposed a timetable on Laurence. She regulated herself of her own accord to the rhythm of a feeding every four hours. From the age of three weeks she never woke me at night. Otherwise I'd never have lasted as far as Tahiti —the goal of this first voyage.

None of it was easy at first. Christian is an excellent sailor, but the best sailor can't prevent his boat from rolling in a heavy swell when there's no wind. I took Marzine four times in forty-eight hours in reduced doses; finally my head cleared a little.

I do everything like an automaton, as if I were drugged. But we're making no headway; we've even stopped praying for Gigi.

"What on earth are we doing in this tub?" Christian smiles. We love our tub, our nest, our *Alpha*. It's just a pity there isn't any wind, that's all.

December 2. Laurence's third day on board the *Alpha*. It's dead calm. The long swell has slowly died down. It's over, and we gradually forget we ever felt sick. Anything we throw overboard keeps pace with us, traveling at a speed of one or two knots in the current. The rigging has stopped clanking. Silence. Schools of dorados, which have come to look at us, play all around us. Laurence is telling us lots of interesting things. Her eyes and head move constantly, punctuated with serious "aa e, aae, aa e" sounds.

However, we can hardly make the crossing using the motor, and we begin to wonder if the wind will ever get up. But the enforced delay does us good. I take advantage of it to dry everything quickly. It's a real pleasure to collect ten dry diapers in one go.

A dead calm is a holiday at sea. The rhythm is broken; the boat is still. The sun enfolds you in its warmth, penetrating everywhere, even below. I get the bedding and clothes out on deck to air in the sun. Sometimes a long swell makes us imagine things, fills our minds with the idea of fantastic underwater monsters, which—in our dreams—could alone explain the slow motion of this inert mass of water. Christian seizes the opportunity to have his one bath of the crossing. I am more prudent. I remember Cindy, a young American girl, who went swimming with her husband in mid-Pacific miles from anywhere. They left their three-year-old son on board, without securing him to anything. When they got back on board the *Sea-Wife* Cindy threw down a bucket for some sea water. It had barely touched the water when two sharks appeared, and one of them carried it off. Cindy hugged her son to her and was cured forever of bathing in mid-ocean.

At last, on the fourth day, there's a light breeze. It's good to feel the water moving past the hull again. No one dares say anything, for fear of frightening the zephyr away. The rigging moves gaily into action. The *Alpha* glides gracefully along like a large white bird. The wind's behind us again. A gentle breath just strong enough to blow us along and give us hope. I begin to look beyond the stove, my baby, and her diapers.

The sky is clear, cloudless. From time to time an adventurous wave breaks on the bow and scatters in a shower of rainbow-colored spray. The sea is a huge living creature, volcanic or lazy. She goes from caresses to a hurricane, from charm to anger. One hardly has time to get an impression of her before she's transformed, replaced by another equally fugitive image. Only a giant camera could capture her moods. I hope the fine weather will last. According to the Casablanca fishermen there's a gale here once a fortnight. We left just after a stormy spell and should reach Las Palmas before the weather breaks again.

From ahead, the *Alpha* looks slender. The wake she leaves in the water adds to the impression of length. At the moment she's moving slowly, at a speed of four knots—the speed of a fast walker. A luxury in this jet age. We will do thousands of miles under our own steam. We're dependent on no one. We can go wherever we like, wherever the wind takes us.

Phosphorescent green dorados appear silhouetted in our wake. They look flat, cut through the water like thrown knives. Suddenly one of them leaps out of the sea, showing its sulfur-yellow belly.

"Christian! A fish!"

The line is stretched taut. The creature fights desperately with

10

great blows of its tail. The rest of the school hurries up and surrounds it curiously, appearing not to understand what's going on. The captain cautiously draws in the line. Only six more feet of nylon to reel in. The dorado looks as though it's tired of fighting. One sharp blow—and hup.

"Damn, it's off the hook."

Goodbye, raw fish à la Tahitienne, grilled fish, fish soup. I mentally put away my frying pan, the oil, the large knife, and it's that damned corned beef again.

Christian sees my disappointment, and says very tenderly: "Look at all the others. We'll catch plenty more."

Day five. We're stricken with flu. We ache all over, with sore heads, throats, and noses, and a fever. Bed. I share mine with Laurence, don't attempt to isolate her. Not a cough. She's growing visibly, full of smiles, which are still uncontrolled. She doesn't even notice the germs we've succumbed to. However, I check my prescriptions and the big chest of baby medicines regularly.

On the sixth day, at midday, the skipper announces that in spite of the small amount of wind during the first few days our daily average is seventy miles, although we're sailing with mainsail alone for lack of a jib boom.

Encouraged by this good news, I wrap up my little parcel warmly and take her up into the cockpit to feed her in the open air. She's snugly installed when a wave breaks violently on the afterdeck, drenching us both. I roar with laughter and cover her little face with kisses as she opens wide, astonished eyes and grimaces at the taste of the salt water. It's a christening of a sort. We stay in the cockpit.

For Laurence, the world, life, is something that moves all the time. The wind, which blows up her nostrils. A bright storm lantern swinging above her head. A perpetual effort, even when she's asleep, to tense her muscles and keep her balance so that she doesn't roll about in her cot. Daddy and Mommy always there.

I'm beginning to feel like a mother. Yet I feel as though I'm ten years old and playing with my dolls. With Christian, I blossomed in the sun, in spite of all our difficulties. And then Laurence arrived—a shining, perfect symbol of our happiness. This seventh day is a gift from heaven. Our flu has gone, and seabirds indicate

11

that land is near. On deck I can savor the mixture of water, sky, and light. The sun warms me through my sweater. My body shivers expectantly.

On the foredeck, which serves as my lookout point, I can feel the boat come alive like an animal breathing, as I sit there. The stem plunges into the water and rises regularly like an animal swimming with its head half submerged, lifting its muzzle now and then to breathe. In this light wind, one can feel the sail about to quiver at the slightest variation in the pressure. And so it could go on for hours, days, months.

Everything one does on a small boat takes a certain time to carry out, which makes you consider it and think it out carefully, and appreciate it at its proper value. For instance, if I'm thirsty, I ask myself first if I really need a drink. I wait until my throat's dry. Then I grip the partition that separates me from the stove, heave myself out of my bunk. After a few acrobatic feats, I've got a glass in my hand. My feet firmly planted against the lockers, I lean on the sink and pump up some of the precious fresh water, which we use only for drinking. I rinse the glass in salt water and put it away immediately. Everything must be in its proper place. The idea of a glass of water has taken on a particular significance, and the same amount of effort goes into each action made throughout the day.

And yet we're drunk with freedom, without quite knowing why we use this word in our cell-like prison. Because it's what we've chosen? "Freedom is the possibility of making one's own decisions," my philosophy professor said. But how many have the courage to choose?

I should add that for us this voyage isn't comparable to a month's holiday on a yacht on the Côte d'Azur. It's not a question of minor discomforts, which the holiday weather soon makes you forget. It's our first experience of the life that we intend to lead for as long as possible, forever perhaps. So each possibility for improvement is carefully noted. Christian is already sketching plans for a new boat. We would like a more comfortable arrangement inside, using the small volume of habitable space to best possible advantage. Each of us dreams quietly, in his own corner, and from time to time a phrase, a word, reveals our common preoccupation: an after cabin with a real double bed; a flush deck or a very flat deck.

12

Every day, after taking our bearings, Christian marks our position on a chart with a little cross. I admire the accuracy of our course: since we left Casablanca the crosses have followed each other in a perfectly straight line in the direction of the Canaries. I'm full of admiration for my skipper, who watches day and night over the boat. He never sleeps deeply. He keeps an eye on the sail, the self-steering gear, and the compass, from his bunk. He's always alert, aware of each part of the boat. He suffers with the mast when it creaks, feels a straining stay like a muscle of his own body. He listens to Gigi and tells himself he must check her bolts. But it's so difficult to get up, so good to lie a little longer in the last rays of the sun, reading one more page.

There's constant noise all around us. The water slides past the hull with a sharp hiss. From time to time a wave breaks loudly on the stem or stern. The whole boat labors. The efforts of the mast, the rigging, the sheets, the self-steering gear join in a cacophony of sound, to which the ear quickly grows accustomed. The captain's on deck immediately if there's any unusual noise or unexpected movement, to find out what's causing it.

But I raise the alarm this time: "Christian! Gigi's bolts have worked loose."

He's on deck immediately, on the afterdeck, clinging with all his might to our precious Gigi, already leaning at an angle of forty-five degrees over the abyss.

"France, the wrench and some wire."

Laurence has woken up and is crying and I yell at the top of my voice: "You be quiet!" Stunned, she shuts up.

We just manage to save the essential part of our automatic steering gear. The bolts had slowly loosened one by one, and a joint had worked loose on the deck.

I go back to the cabin. There's a strange noise of trickling water.

"Christian. Quick! Water's coming into the boat. Hurry!"

"Find some corks, grease, rags. It's the holes in the hull we made to fasten on the self-steering gear. The bolts aren't there now."

Luckily everything's in the kitchen drawer.

Christian doesn't panic at all. I'm almost in tears. Reproaches spring to my lips. The water's coming in and I imagine Laurence drowning.

Suspended in a bosun's chair, his body in the icy water, Christian stops the holes one by one, while I take the tiller. The big blue-and-white towel is ready on the cockpit bench to dry him. But I have the awful habit, at such moments, of thinking about those great fish.

At last it's all over. It's growing dark. We just have time to see what we imagine is the Canary Island of Lanzarote, just visible in the mist to the southwest. While I prepare some split peas with corned beef, Christian hurriedly tries to mend our helmsman. He looks at the land, the horizon: "If all goes well, it should be hot showers and steak tomorrow."

We smile, Christian a bit uneasily, as he feels responsible for the accident with Gigi. He should have checked before. It was careless of him. What is this feebleness that seems to attack everyone at sea? On a yacht, in mid-ocean, you try to save your strength as much as possible, because a lot of energy is used up involuntarily, just by the motion of the boat.

The sun goes down and I ask timidly: "Shall we take watches? I'll help if you like."

"No, I'll secure the tiller and stream the log so we'll know how much distance we've made. We're bound to drift a bit."

The wind has dropped. We go to sleep. In the night, the wind frequently changes direction, and we end up sailing close-hauled. Christian keeps getting up. There's no light on the horizon, which is odd. Each time the wind changes, we half wake and remember that land isn't far off and that we no longer have a functioning Gigi to take us there. Will it take one day? Two days? The hours slowly pass, punctuated only by the rocking of the *Alpha*.

Next day at dawn I feed Laurence on deck, while the sun comes up behind us like a great ball of fire on the horizon.

Christian puts on the kettle for breakfast and looks at the log: "Only fourteen miles. And we've drifted a lot."

There is a following wind again. It has freshened and makes us want to make up the lost ground. Christian puts on his yellow oilskin: "I'll take the tiller for a while."

I bring him some breakfast—a rusk and butter and some tea.

14

Lanzarote is no longer in sight. We set course for Las Palmas. We're still sailing under mainsail alone. It's 64 degrees—spring heat. From her crib in the bottom of the cockpit Laurence gazes out. She's growing so fast. I love seeing Christian's smile on her lips.

2

A Difficult Course

I think back to my own childhood. My parents lived in Tahiti—my father of French and Spanish background, my mother of French, Russian, and probably Madagascan heritage. My father was self-educated, a soldier when he was stationed in Tahiti, where he met my mother. Later they lived in France, where I was born in 1942. They had suffered a great deal during the war—my father fought with the Resistance—and after the war returned to live in Tahiti with my brother, my sister, and me.

It was a very strict family and I can remember many quarrels and arguments, constant surveillance. Life had been very hard for them; they were exiles and extremely lonely, and poverty had been no stranger to them for many years. But I knew that I would never want to treat my children as they had us. There was a climate of

16

mutual distrust between parents and children. I concentrated very hard on my studies so I could win a scholarship to study in France, where I spent three years at an Ursuline school. Later I studied physics in Lyon. Intellectually I was advanced, reading, listening to music, turned inward, not knowing if I was European or Tahitian. Emotionally, however, I was very immature and inexperienced.

When I got back to Tahiti with all my degree certificates, I was the perfect old maid. I got a job as an inspector for the new Post Office Bank. I was very good at it, a real electronic brain, remembering everyone's account easily. But I had to live at home with my parents and they treated me like a child, even though I was twenty-one. They allowed me ten minutes to get home from work. If I was late, if I stopped to gossip with a friend, they interrogated me. It was impossible.

When I met Christian, my friends pitied me for being kept a prisoner by my family. I had one good friend, François, who secretly introduced me to night life in Tahiti. We loved to talk about intellectual things. It was with François that I met Christian, at a nightclub. Christian asked me to dance. In his arms I felt like a child in the arms of a grownup. Safe. He told me I had lovely eyes, a banal phrase that moved me deeply, for I had always been told I was ugly. When we remember our first meeting Christian recalls a violent and immediate physical attraction. I don't, but can I trust memory?

François, Christian, and I became inseparable—three friends, but all very different. Christian seemed to me to be a playboy, deeply tanned, who roared around in his red sports car, making money by taking instant snapshots of tourists in the harbor, at parties. I fell in love without being aware of it. I was bewildered, in the hands of fate.

We had met in April. We didn't make love until July. My saner self told me Christian was not the boy for me, two years younger, no regular job, changing girls as fancy took him. But he was like a drug I couldn't live without. It was Christian I loved. And, since he wanted to take me and carry me away, I would go with him, no matter where, no matter how. I would obey his instincts.

Christian spent his childhood being passed from one boarding school to another. Born in Paris, he was separated early from his mother. He was the eldest of five brothers, but they never lived as a family. He remembers with great emotion the holidays he spent with his grandfather near Boulogne; he loved the stormy sea, the long walks on deserted beaches, fishing. They were the only times he felt part of a clan he could be proud of.

After his military service, Christian found himself in New Caledonia—handsome, fit, no money, few qualifications for work. He had dreamed of going to Tahiti since childhood and leaped at the chance of getting there. Doing odd jobs, he had managed to buy himself a red Fiat sports car and, being "new" in Tahiti, he attracted a lot of attention. He began taking snapshots to sell to the tourists. He covered the nightclubs, photographing people on their vacations. Every night he counted his money and put it in the bank. Life seemed not to be so difficult after all. And just before meeting me he met a boat—the *Carmellia,* owned by two Americans who were sailing around the world. For one who had never been to sea except on a passenger boat, it was a great discovery. To live on a boat . . . to sail away, to discover an island . . . to break free of everything, from memories of childhood restrictions, boarding schools . . . it was a way of using all one's abilities. When they asked Christian to come with them as crew, he accepted enthusiastically —a new life of adventure stretching out before him. It was then, as I sat with François at the nightclub talking about Teilhard de Chardin, he asked me to dance. . . .

My escape from my family was like a detective story. As every-one knows everything in Tahiti, I had to use cunning. I wrote to a friend on another island to ask her to telephone the Postmaster General, for whom I worked, and ask if I could have a fortnight's leave to go and stay with her. Naturally, the Postmaster telephoned my parents. This ruse was vital, because if I had told the truth my father would have done everything he could to stop me.

Every morning I took a little parcel of things with me, gradu-ally emptying my closets. On the last day, when I was supposed to be taking a boat to go to my friend's island, I knew I would never be coming home again. I had been unhappy, it was true, and yet I felt sad. I looked for a moment at all my father's records and books, and could only remember the few happy times. My child-hood and youth had been filled with music. It woke us up in the

18

morning, and soared around us all day. It was hard to tell where silence ended and music began; each was as exquisite, as dense as the other. And the books. There were more than three thousand in the house; I slept in their midst. We were all great readers, but my mother held the record for quantity. Outside was our wilderness, great tall trees which I had climbed to study or meditate for hours. The sky, the coconut palms. At other times I lay in the soft green grass, gazed at the sky through the palm fronds, by day or night, by moonlight or in the dark. All Tahiti rose up before me, and my throat was tight with tears, on the threshold of this house I was leaving.

I hid in the hold of the *Carmellia*. Until the last moment I was terrified that my father would get wind of something and arrive at the harbor to stop us from leaving. Christian waited until we were out at sea before letting me out of my hiding place. We were sailing westward, toward New Zealand. Later, I wrote to my parents, saying that I was staying on at my friend's for another fortnight. After a month, they realized what had happened: they had discovered I had taken all my things. My father went to ask the police to get me back. But as I was well over adult age all he could do was rage. My childhood was over.

We spent seven months in the Society Islands, cruising from one bay to another. Seven hard months for me, who as a "crew member sharing expenses" spent most of the time cooking and cleaning. Luckily there were the beaches, the marvelously clear water where Christian could indulge his passion for underwater fishing. I didn't fish but I swam alongside him.

We gradually realized that the *Carmellia* could hardly have been a worse boat. The black hull was rotten, patched up with cement. There was every reason to be scared. On the night of my flight we had nearly sunk. As the sun was very hot, and black a much hotter color than white, when the planks dried they cracked and parted; you could see daylight through them on the waterline. When we heeled over the boat began to fill. We had to bail all night, because, naturally, neither the electric pump nor the hand pump worked. We paddled about in the dark—there was no electricity—stumbling and being sick, and wishing that we could die. Finally, at dawn, we saw an island. If we hadn't succeeded in reaching it we would have died, because the boat was still filling in spite of our exhausted efforts. I didn't want to abandon Christian, but it was hardly an auspicious start to my sailing career.

The holes in the *Carmellia* were filled with cement and painted. But the rotten wood continued to come away bit by bit. Give me a steel hull any day.

I was frightened in the water. It was Christian who taught me to know the sea. When he swam he was completely happy and relaxed, and I gradually learned to feel the same, to forget the childish fear and inhibitions that made the water appear dangerous, treacherous. I learned to let myself go like a fetus in the dark blue depths of the bays, to forge straight ahead without thinking of possible dangers, to communicate with the watery element. To swim like that is sheer delight. When you are afraid you project your fears. Thanks to Christian, I gradually got over this.

Sometimes my fears return in these mysterious bays: without a mask you open your eyes and see cloudy water. That great fish could be a tuna, or a barracuda, or a shark. The spell is broken; you swim away at a fast crawl, as quickly as you can.

Christian knows sharks. He respects them. They respect him. He's no more afraid of them than he is of dogs. And they don't attack without cause. The only accidents I've seen in Polynesia have been when a fisherman was cleaning a fish that bled into the water, while he had a leg in the sea. The shark comes to get the fish and bites off the leg with it. They might also bite underwater fisherman who attaches his fish to his belt, as they do in France. Or a shipwrecked swimmer becomes exhausted, and the shark smells that he's in a weak state. Like all Polynesian fishermen, Christian trails his fish at the end of a long line. If the shark wants the fish, he can take it without going near the man. If you're fit, and not afraid, sharks won't attack you—as a rule.

After seven months, Christian and I returned to the Tahitian harbor town of Papeete. Christian, who had learned a lot about the sea on the *Carmellia*, looked around at the harbor. And he saw the *Walborg*, a gigantic fore-and-aft schooner, which had been a Baltic cargo ship for eighty years. A young Swede, Böse, had bought it for a song, and refitted it. He remade all the sails himself, by hand, hundreds and hundreds of square yards of them, made of cotton.

Nothing on the boat was modern: no bottle screws but dead-eyes from the time of Christopher Columbus. A huge square sail, which you no longer see, but which is very effective in following winds.

The boys were looking for a crewman, but didn't want a girl: it was hard enough sailing this great boat anyway. Christian went alone. I was to join him later, in New Zealand.

I felt very lost when the *Walborg* sailed majestically out of the harbor. I was alone in Tahiti. I couldn't see my family, and I thought I might never see Christian again.

Christian learned a lot on the *Walborg* from these four boys, who had already been everywhere. They were great blond creatures, real Vikings. At least half the day was taken up with deck work: emptying the bilges, sluicing the deck to keep it damp enough, mending sails, scraping the bowsprit and the masts, fighting the constant wear and tear.

The engine never worked. Luckily the skipper, Böse, was an incomparable sailor. Christian later told me admiringly about their arrival in Raïatea. The island is surrounded by coral: you go into a bottleneck and then find yourself in the lagoon, which is only six hundred feet wide. But the boat was speeding on. How do you turn, in a following wind, without an engine, when you know how much maneuvering space is needed by the *Walborg?* They were sailing at full speed. They had to give way, and turn from sailing with the wind dead astern, into the wind, because the coral reef was directly in front of them The tiller was no use alone. Böse let out the foresails, and the *Walborg* literally turned on the spot. "It was incredible," Christian told me. "That great bulk, and going so fast. We were saved."

They finally reached New Zealand. It was Christian's first long ocean crossing. It was then that he learned to navigate by the stars. He was never idle: as he was the most agile it was always he who had to climb up the mast, when necessary. One day the tail of a typhoon hit the *Walborg,* when Christian was on the squaresail yard. He still doesn't quite know how he managed not to fall off. The voyage lasted three months.

When Christian found himself on land once more, he felt an unaccustomed buoyancy and strength. He felt as though the world belonged to him. What an extraordinary drug you find you have within yourself, and the sea releases. Nothing is impossible when you achieve such command of your body.

In Auckland the crew split up. Each went his own way. Christian had already written to me from their ports of call; letters full of love and enthusiasm. He wrote from Auckland telling me to join him. When I arrived in Auckland, neither of us had any money. But Christian told me firmly: "I know how to sail. I've learned enough now to know that I want my own boat."

From that day on, we lived with the idea of getting a boat. To make some money we started to work in a big store. I sold cosmetics and Christian was in stock control.

"If you go to evening classes," we were told, "you'll get ahead."

Well, yes. But an employee's life wasn't much fun. Christian with his packing cases, and I standing behind my counter all day. At the end of the week we got our pay: according to the law of the land, mine was half that of Christian's, because I was a woman. I wouldn't stand for it, and Christian backed me up. So we took our money and stalked out of the shop by the main door as if we were customers. It was marvelous to be in the street again. We strolled along completely happy and carefree.

And we found ourselves in a Pan-American plane on our way back to Tahiti. We decided it was the only place we knew where we could gather the funds to buy our first boat—our *Alpha*.

We arrived in Tahiti at ten in the morning in brilliant sunshine. We both had one aim, one idea only: to get the money to buy a yacht.

We got a room at the cheapest hotel in Papeete, and put our rucksack in the corner of the room. We hired a scooter, and bought two Polaroid cameras and a box of film, all on credit. We told ourselves: "Now all Tahiti belongs to us. In a few weeks, or months, we'll buy our boat."

It was June. We worked day and night for six months without a break. We had to win—to get our first boat, achieve the first most difficult step, starting from scratch to get the 50,000 new francs we would need.

We exploited the instant-photo field methodically, relentlessly. It was a gold mine. Arrivals and departures at the airport. Film stars

22

mingling with the crowds, the new arrivals being rapturously greeted. A holiday mood, with flowers everywhere. At each arrival or departure of a plane the whole island is there, with music playing, and the scene is charged with emotion. Everyone wants a photograph. In this relaxed, friendly, happy, and carefree atmosphere, where life is one long holiday, with dancing and singing, we worked to the rhythm of our cameras—click, click, click.

And the money poured in. To keep up this frenetic pace, we had rented a comfortable house. We bought a car, an extra camera each, electronic flashes: in view of the money that came in it was sensible to invest. So as not to run out of film, we bought it by the crateload. We ate a lot of raw fish and fruit to make up for our lack of sleep, because we were at all the celebrations, every night.

In the harbor we saw the great sailors, Moitessier, Deshumeurs, Paul Smet, and others, on board their seabirds, their steel-hulled boats—and our boat took shape: it would be a steel-hulled sloop about twenty-eight feet long. Christian wrote to all the shipyards.

Our nerves began to get ragged with all the work. To relax, we went swimming. There, stretched on the sand, we didn't talk about getting married, or children, but only about boats. And one day Christian said, almost solemnly: "We've got just enough to buy the boat. I've had a reply from a Dutch boatyard, at Dokkum. I'm going to go there to order it."

I would have to spend four months alone in Tahiti again.

A few days after Christian left, I realized I was pregnant.

Having put down the first installment in Dokkum, Christian went to the Côte d'Azur. He was looking for second-hand gear for his first boat: charts, a sextant, anchors. He met an American on a forty-two-foot teak schooner, which he had had built in Hong Kong. He needed a crewman to go to Hawaii. Christian couldn't go that far: he wanted to oversee the building of the boat, he had further installments to pay, and he had to hunt around like a scrap dealer for all the second-hand gear. When the boat had been paid for, there would be very little money left over for sailing it, and a new sextant costs 2,000 francs, a chart 10 francs—and you need hundreds of them—an anchor 1,000 francs, and so on.

"That doesn't matter," said the American. "I've got a fast boat.

We'll go as far as Gibraltar. I'll drop you off there and you can take the train to Amsterdam to go and see your boat, pay the second installment, etc. You can then join me by plane—I'll pay for everything—we'll cross the Atlantic, and you can come back by plane.

Which was what they did. Christian recruited his brother Didier as crew, and while the boat was being built, he had the pleasure of crossing the Atlantic, picking up the gear he wanted on the way.

Meanwhile, when he had returned Paris, he had received the letter telling him I was pregnant. I cried when I read Christian's enthusiastic letter: he was wild with joy and told me to join him in France immediately. I was numb with surprise. I had been sure he would be upset, as it hadn't entered into our scheme. We had thought only of a boat. I sold all the camera equipment and got on the first passenger steamer.

"I've never been more in love with you," he told me, "than when I saw you walking down the gangplank in your white minidress with your little stomach."

The arrival of the steamer from Tahiti in Marseille is a moving sight. Tahitian families living in France, so far from their homeland in the sun, come to meet their friends and relatives, whose brown skins remind them of the sea and the palm trees.

We arrived in Dokkum with our rucksack, two bowls, two plates, and the money to pay the final installment on the boat. At the north of the canal we saw our *Alpha*—gleaming white. We held hands like children. We couldn't believe it.

A solemn moment. Christian took the tiller of his first boat, the first boat of his own. Until then he had sailed as a crew, had obeyed orders. And now he was the skipper, and a father-to-be, but for the moment, naturally, he couldn't be expected to think of anything but this white bird, already skimming toward the sea.

In three months we had crossed Europe along the canals. We were eager to hoist the sails, but had to wait until the Mediterranean. Holland, Belgium, France. On the Seine we nearly lost the *Alpha*. In a lock, our propeller got caught in some ropes; we couldn't move. An enormous barge was descending on us. This mass, with its engines stopped, was still making way and couldn't

24

stop. The lock loudspeakers were going mad telling us to clear the way. The siren howled. Christian dived into the pea soup of dead rats, which is what the Seine is outside Paris, and succeeded in extricating the propeller at the last moment. I was in tears of despair: our brand-new *Alpha*. Christian managed to slam her against the side, and the barge passed with a few inches to spare.

We were towed to immediately opposite the Île Saint-Louis. We stayed there a month: Christian had to mend the propeller. Then we set off once more, longing to be on the open sea.

The Canal de Bourgogne was very calm, but going down the Rhône was quite another matter. It's a very turbulent river, strewn with gravel beds, rocks, and whirlpools. We should have taken on a pilot at Lyon, but it was too expensive. We had entered on our period of frantic economizing.

"We've got to get as far as Tahiti," Christian said.

Rationing was strict.

When we got to the Camargue—a foretaste of the Amazon— there were no more buoys. With the combined speed of the current and the engine Christian hardly had time to read the references on the charts, instructions such as "Keep within 45 feet of the bank," or "Head for the right bank at an angle of 45 degrees," or "Keep at a distance of 30 feet from the right bank," or "Steer over to port again." It is essential to follow these instructions carefully to avoid the shoals. If you don't follow them inch by inch the boat is lost.

At Port-Saint-Louis we were amazed at the sight of the turbulent Rhône flowing into the sea, the shore covered with wreckage and deadwood. Twisted branches, old packing cases, toys lost by children on a nearby beach, no doubt packed with bodies now in August. But we sailed out to sea. We raised the masts, hoisted the sails. The second solemn moment since Christian took the tiller of the *Alpha* in Dokkum: our white bird spread her wings.

We were heading for Saint-Tropez, because Christian's godmother owned a small vineyard near there, at Luc-en-Provence, and we had to start thinking about somewhere to be while I had the baby: time was running short.

I was eight months pregnant when we got married at Pégomas, near Cannes, where Christian's father is a doctor. An elderly American couple whom we met at the last minute acted as witnesses. They gave us our only wedding presents. We were on our own and it was completely informal: I wore a miniskirt and one of Christian's shirts.

Until October, we "tried out" the *Alpha* in the Mediterranean; then there was the wine harvest at the vineyard. I cooked and washed up for the men, while Christian helped with the grape gathering—we needed the money. Our baby was born in Brignoles, on October 18, 1967.

Three days after Laurence was born, Christian decided to go as far as Casablanca with his brother Didier, so that the *Alpha* could cross the Mediterranean before winter. The Mediterranean is the most dangerous of all seas, particularly in winter. They would steer a direct course toward Casablanca, via the Balearic Islands, Almería and Gibraltar. It felt very strange being left on my own with such a small baby—my first. I was anxious to rejoin them at Casablanca, especially as a letter from Christian, posted in the Balearics, was most enthusiastic about all the *Alpha*'s good points. I used the 400 francs Christian had left me sparingly, so that I would be able to pay my fare on the steamer *Ancerville*—which would be 280 francs. I had to live for a fortnight in Luc on the remaining 120 francs, and then take a train to Marseille. And what would I do on arrival in Casablanca? Christian had only been able to give me a rough idea of when he would get there.

However, tired as I was after the birth, I didn't want to wait any longer. In Marseille Christian's family didn't want me to set out with Laurence. I was amazed to hear them call him an irresponsible wretch, and tell me that I shouldn't join him but stay in France, where they would help me. But, in spite of my tiredness, and all the difficulties, something precious bound me to Christian; it was not the moment to give in. I arrived in Casablanca with 20 francs in my pocket. I was keeping them to buy a present for Christian.

The yacht club where the *Alpha* was supposed to have arrived was a good way off. I didn't know what taxis cost, and didn't want to risk taking one in case I couldn't pay. So I walked. Seeing me walking along with my baby on my arm, taxi drivers drew up beside me. I shook my head. Finally one of them said: "I'll take you—you needn't pay." So I got in. I'll never forget this kind gesture.

Christian was there, and our *Alpha* was rocking gently in front of the boat club. I was full of emotion at the thought that it would be our house, our home.

We were often told that she seemed larger inside than out. She is twenty-eight feet long, about eight feet wide and draws almost five feet of water. You can stand up inside, fore and aft. With her steel hull, there is height belowdecks even in the forecastle, where there is a double bunk. We used this only when in port. The door of the washroom can then be opened to separate us completely from the saloon. This has two large bunks, which we use at sea, and a long box bunk, which goes under the cockpit, in the stern on the starboard side. In Casablanca Christian was collecting provisions for the crossing, and the box bunk was covered with sacks of potatoes and onions. Laurence slept at my feet on the port side, on my bunk. The stove and sink were at the head of the bunk. We had about ten square feet to move around in, around the folding table. The cupboard was opposite the washroom. A good light was assured by extra-large portholes, which could be protected by steel shutters if necessary.

I stared at the *Alpha* admiringly as if I had never seen her before. All white inside and out, except for the inner planking and a few panels of polished mahogany. I found her at Casablanca still beautifully white. Christian had taken advantage of the low tide to repaint the waterline. But she already bore the scars of a rough passage. The beautiful polished mast was pitted from the storm that Christian and Didier had run into off Ibiza.

The seasons impose a timetable on us. The passage to Tahiti is the same for all boats that want to take advantage of a warm tropical temperature and the trade winds, and to reduce the risk of hurricanes and bad weather. You must leave the Mediterranean before the end of autumn and get beyond the Atlantic coast of Morocco. The best time to go from the Canaries to the West Indies is between October and March. Then you must leave the West Indies before the northern summer, so as to avoid tropical storms, which are frequent in these parts toward the middle of the year. And in the Pacific it is a good idea to get to French Polynesia before the hot season, which begins in November and may also have heavy storms.

I longed to pack a rucksack and go to Marrakech. But it isn't a good idea to leave your boat in the harbor while you go very far inland. If a mooring line or an anchor is stolen the boat will drift away. If the harbor is not well sheltered, a gust of wind can slam her up against the quay.

The time of year, the dangers of a boat alone in port were ideal reasons to leave Casablanca as soon as possible. Or more precisely to reach the West Indies as soon as possible. Christian admitted later that he wouldn't really believe his dream had come true until he could drop anchor from his own boat in a turquoise lagoon, fringed with white sand and coconut palms.

We stayed in Casablanca for only three days, during which we explored the old Medina. Between feedings we wandered through the Arab quarter like lovers. Surrounded by veils and trailing robes I felt naked in my miniskirt. Stalls of everything one could possibly eat overflowed onto pavements in little heaps or pyramid-like mounds. I tasted sweetmeats dripping with honey. There was a strong smell of spices, mixed with that of the sea and of patchouli. I noticed the way women carried their babies on their backs. But Laurence was asleep on the boat, because Christian had assured me souks were the breeding ground for every imaginable germ.

We got in the rest of our supplies. Christian haggled every-where. The stall holders seemed to expect it. To do otherwise would have disappointed them.

One could live on almost nothing in Casablanca, which was fortunate considering the state of our purse when we bought our provisions. I still have a careful list that the skipper made in the log book.

12 large loaves of bread	0.30 francs each
10 pounds of oranges	0.30 francs for two pounds
3 dozen eggs	1.60 a dozen
2 pounds of fresh butter	3.00 francs

All vegetables, whether fresh or dried, were five or ten centimes a couple of pounds. We have often thought about that list since. The abject poverty that surrounded us inspired a desire to help the people get out of there and at the same time to take to our heels. But not pity, because they were very proud, and very dignified. I admire these people, who have managed to keep their traditions intact in spite of the modern European civilization, which is firmly installed on their doorstep. As soon as you leave the market, Casablanca is an ultra-modern town, with luxury flats and wide streets. The Arabs slip unobtrusively along, adapt, and continue to live their dignified lives, remaining completely Moroccan.

Casablanca is also the yacht club, with its visitors' book that you leaf through, eagerly looking for the names of those who have set out before you. Each yacht that passes through is invited by the sailing club to leave its name, accompanied by a photograph if possible. We found several boats there that we had seen in Tahiti, in particular the *Vencia* belonging to Pierre and Catherine Deshumeurs and Bernard and Françoise Moitessier's *Joshua.* We were careful to note particulars of our own voyage, including our extra "hand," Laurence. A solemn ritual, which made us feel we were joining the band of great sailors. It's the last message one leaves at any port, before setting out for the unknown, toward death perhaps: because the sea is merciless.

Casablanca also means Loïck Fougeron, a good friend to all sailors. A little enigmatic, he is always there when you need a helping hand, source of invaluable information for getting a repair done, or having automatic steering gear fitted.

Casablanca is the concrete sink at the foot of the yacht club steps I monopolized every morning, plunging my hands into the icy water. I had imagined all kinds of difficult situations before Laurence was born, but not washing diapers.

Casablanca is all the yachts that were leaving at the same time as we were for the West Indies. They were all talking of voyaging round the world, a dream that sometimes comes true but that is satisfying in itself. Of twenty boats that year, we would be the only one to reach Tahiti. We had traveled around the world several times already, with the help of a plane or seaplane here, a steamer or someone else's boat there. Now we were in our own cockleshell, going back to Tahiti in search of sun and desert islands; to work there for a while. I was well aware that we had not primarily chosen this life because of "the call of the sea." It was because we knew no profession that would enable us to live in a town in a house with a garden, a swimming pool or the sea nearby, skiing or riding available, and a life style that would give us time to see each other and our children.

It was to preserve our family life, living in the natural surroundings we loved, and to satisfy our desire for travel, that we chose a solution within our reach: a small boat. It was our seaborne minicar, our gypsy wagon.

We ran into some friends at the yacht club. On Jean-Claude Brouillet's *Erna,* a superb and beautifully painted fifty-six-foot ketch, we found Eric Deschamps, who had lost the *Railleuse* on a reef in the Tuamotu Archipelago—the Danger Islands.

The *Erna* had just come into the harbor. The rattling of a chain being let out attracted our attention. A few minutes later a Zodiac put out, and I shouted: "Eric!"

Christian dived and swam rapidly toward him.

"Good heavens," Eric said, "you here! Is that your boat? And baby? I've got one hour to get in some supplies before we leave. Rendezvous at Las Palmas."

Just like that. What more natural than to make a rendezvous for a spot a few hundred miles away. In a good wind.

On the *Mamari,* a twenty-eight-foot sloop, we found Ken and Marie. On the *Ain-Taiba,* the Valin brothers: they had had it built as a modified version of the *Joshua.* They had constructed the interior themselves. While Henri explained the advantages of a vegetarian diet to me, I watched a six-year-old child playing on the deck of the *Anahita.*

There was no time to get to know the other boats that, under flags of every color, stopped only long enough to restock with provisions. But we would meet the *Solmar* with her varnished hull and the *Rhâ* with her Swiss flag later on.

The meteorological office announced that the storm we had heard about had died down at sea. The wind had moderated. The others had already set sail for the Canaries. It was vital to leave at once; and on November 30 we set sail at about ten o'clock. Loïck had given our automatic steering gear, our beloved Gigi, a final inspection, and had shaken his head doubtfully. On the jetty, where several members of the yacht club had gathered, a forty-year-old

30

paterfamilias made a last attempt to convince us of the folly of our undertaking.

"You don't have to go. Spend the winter here and give the baby a chance to grow a bit."

And they made the suggestion that was made at every port, without fail: "Leave her with us: we'll send her on by plane as soon as you're safely across."

Leave my daughter? She was part of our adventure. Loïck threw us the last mooring line, and I took the tiller while the skipper hoisted the jib. We never use the engine if it can be avoided.

The wind filled the canvas. A furrow of white foam sprang up in our wake. I loved hearing the "flip, flap" as the sail unfurled. The *Alpha* flew on, with her wings spread wide, irresistibly drawn toward the open sea, or *moana* as it is called in Tahitian.

Christian repeated his anti-seasickness prescription: "Drink plenty of water, eat well, wrap up so you don't get cold, and rest as much as you can." A marvelous program.

Christian was at the helm. I stretched myself out at his feet, on the cockpit seat, to feed Laurence.

3

Christmas at Sea

The tenth day. Nightfall, and there is a light directly ahead of us. Four flashes every thirty seconds—Las Palmas. Land, wonderful land lies ahead. Our friends will have arrived already and must be worrying about us.

While I sleep Christian steers us toward the shore. It takes all night. At breakfast, at about six, I find him exhausted from lack of sleep but smiling radiantly: "Look." In front of us, under heavy rain clouds, lies Las Palmas.

We are very excited, and deliriously happy to have completed the first ten-day crossing alone with our baby. We suddenly realize everything that might have happened—a storm, and heavy seas with Laurence being sick. We're delighted that we're all three alive and in good shape. We begin to understand that to be alive is not to be dead, not to be lost overboard.

Another yacht, a little ahead of us, is also sailing toward Las Palmas. As it's raining we can't make it out very clearly. It has two masts and its rigging looks like that of Bernard Moitessier's *Joshua.* Or is it the *Ain-Taiba,* with Didier on board? No, it can't be. The *Ain-Taiba* should have arrived long ago. It's obviously using its engine. That's the only thing to do with so little wind and the endless rain.

At seven Christian starts the engine. A good little ten-horse-power diesel, which, with much putting from its one cylinder, brought the *Alpha* twenty-five hundred miles across Europe by river and canal. For an hour and a half, in the rain that trickles under our oilskins, we try to make some headway, make up for lost time.

At midday we're still at sea and the sun still isn't showing itself. Christian starts the engine again, and at about four o'clock we reach Las Palmas harbor, where there is a heavy swell. Laurence's diapers bedizen the guardrails.

The *Ain-Taiba* got in this morning; it had been she we saw earlier. There's a piercing whistle—Didier signaling to us to come alongside. There's not very much room in the harbor, even for a small boat. You can't see the jetties. Cargo ships and Japanese fishing boats berth there permanently. The only corner we can see is a long way from the center of the town, and with dust blowing over it in thick clouds. Finally, having fixed the fenders, I throw the mooring lines to Didier.

"I was very worried not to find you here when I arrived this morning," he says. "With Laurence. Then I thought perhaps it was you we saw early this morning. How is my goddaughter and niece?"

"Fine," said Christian. "We didn't have any wind the first few days. It was maddening. The day before yesterday Gigi worked loose. But we managed. We didn't take watches because there wasn't any rush. How did you get on? I thought you'd be here long ago."

"We got off course. I don't think the sextant was properly adjusted. We hugged the coast as far as Agadir. We took exactly the same time as you did."

Obviously a day or two either way doesn't matter to us. The

main thing is not to tire ourselves out unnecessarily. There is no cozy house waiting for us at the other end where we can build up our strength. If you want to live face to face with nature like this for any length of time you must respect her laws. So we discipline ourselves to go to bed and get up with the sun all year round: in the Tropics we have twelve hours' sleep. We don't eat highly spiced or much cooked food. Vegetables are eaten raw or steamed in their skins in salt water. We don't drink coffee, or even tea, or any alcoholic drinks.

After ten days of healthy existence on the open sea, the polluted, foggy air that surrounds us here gets us down. Las Palmas is abominably dirty. The water is covered with a disgusting layer of thick black oil, and anything dropped overboard is completely unusable.

From the quay the boats are moored as follows: three cargo ships alongside one another, a fishing smack, the beautiful *Erna*, the *Ain-Taiba* and the *Alpha*. It won't be easy going ashore with the baby. But we're delighted to find Ken, Eric, and all the crew of the *Ain-Taiba* with their guitars, singing to the frenzied beat of *"des sous, des sous, c'est ça qui nous rend fous."*

They rush up to look at our small deckhand, with her plump little dimpled face. Laurence smiles happily and gazes inquiringly at them. Ken shakes his head, thinking of Marie, who will join him in Barbados, in the south of the lesser Antilles.

"You're crazy," says Jean-Claude Brouillet. "But I don't know. They'll be the happiest years of your life."

Eric, who is wondering behind his heavy horn-rimmed spectacles how one can find a mere "digestive tract" interesting, suddenly sees the attraction, and photographs her from every angle.

When we've seen to the boat, Jean-Claude invites us to dinner. It's a welcome break after ten days at sea, and our day-long efforts to make our way in the rain into this dirty, windswept harbor.

On the *Erna*, where the décor, music, and laughter remind us of Tahiti and the sun, we can forget for a while that it's only fifty degrees in our cabin, and that we have no shower or washing machine or running water. On this superb yacht, where everyone has his own washbasin, with running hot water, I gaze longingly at all the refinements. I am amazed to think that it was all part of my life once—three years ago. I realize that never again will I have all those little things that make a woman's life easier. But I'm happy.

Jean-Claude gives us ten rolls of color film and a strong safety belt, so we'll have a color souvenir of our first long voyage together. And, thanks to the safety harness, I won't be afraid when Christian goes to set a storm sail up forward.

Our stop at Las Palmas is purely utilitarian. We need to take on supplies for the Atlantic crossing and repair the automatic pilot. But the port has nothing to offer a small boat. We have to cross six other boats to reach the jetty.

The town of Las Palmas is very spread out, as we soon find from our long daily treks to get our mail. Every day we go to the yacht club, a mile and a half from the harbor. The main post office is even farther and there are letters waiting for us there, as well as in the harbor master's office. Letters are very important to us at sea. They are the only means of keeping in touch with friends and relatives, and those we send are as precious as those we receive. Three weeks without any news can sometimes cause one's family to be worried enough to send out search parties.

Las Palmas is a typical tourist resort, with its smiling, wheedling poverty; you never know if someone's going to do you a favor or swindle you. In its duty-free shops you find cheap walkie-talkie sets, cameras, and radios, together with every kind of souvenir in wood or plastic. Another—rather special—tourist item: boys and girls of sixteen to twenty-two from Scandinavia or the States, roaming the world and living haphazardly. On a beautiful beach fringed with palm trees, like an illustration in a travel agent's brochure, there is a notice saying: LEAVE YOUR LEFTOVER FOOD HERE. Parties of rich tourists descend on the beach to picnic. When the visitors have gone, a beautifully tanned, bearded youth or a blonde Swedish girl comes and collects the food. "It's quite simple," a young American tells me. He has come to live there for a month in a hut he has built on the beach. "When a steamer comes in, all the passengers get off armed with a little lunch basket supplied by the ship. There's always too much food. Why throw it away? They're embarrassed, and delighted to see the notice."

35

When these youngsters grow tired of the place, they try to sail on elsewhere aboard one of the many yachts that call in at Las Palmas.

The town is very Spanish. Beautiful smooth golden skins that hide hunger and poverty. Shy faces revealing a warm sensuality. Incessant chatter, and great dignity of manner.

For the last three days Christian has been mending the rudder of the self-steering gear himself, using the workshop of a local carpenter, who is kindly letting him borrow tools and wood. I've seen the rudder blade. It's thick, and heavier than the last one, which split. I hope Gigi will soon be mended. I feel as though we've lost a part of ourselves. Then she's back—with the sun. We slip the mooring lines. En route for Fuerteventure—Gigi's back and we must try her out. Didier, tempted by the thought of underwater fishing, jumps aboard with his kit, which he throws into the forecastle.

Contrary to all logic, we are sailing with a head wind. It's fun. At nightfall the wind drops. There is an almost full moon and we sing on deck until about midnight to warm ourselves up. The *Alpha* drifts peacefully on till dawn. We laze about for two days and the boys fish. At Lobos, where we drop anchor in a stormy bay, there are some small cubelike bungalows surrounded by white rocks and sand for tourists who like the desert. The barrenness is alleviated by a solitary palm tree. One wonders how it got there.

A strong east wind takes us back to Las Palmas, where it is gray and raining again.

December 22. Where will we spend Christmas? No one dares ask, and the question hangs over us, oppressive as the lowering gray sky, depressing as the endless drizzle, which prevents drying the washing. I was hoping for a decorated tree for Laurence, and mountains of presents. She's just two months old.

I wash and wash, pumping up the fresh water. I've counted: it takes twelve strokes of the pump to get a kettleful, twenty-four for a bowlful, forty-seven to wash and twice forty-seven, that is ninety-four, to rinse. It's maddening. Especially when you've got to bend over the sink.

And it's nearly Christmas. I'm miserable. I haven't got any presents to give. When I got to Casablanca, Christian asked me if

36

I had any money left. I had hidden away my remaining 20 francs in an envelope, under Laurence's mattress, so that I could get presents for Christian, Laurence, and Didier—just small presents. But he asked me if I had any money because he hadn't any cash for the stores. And I handed it over miserably, without saying anything.

I was broken-hearted. Christmas was spoiled: it wouldn't be Christmas for me. It's especially hard when you've got a baby two months old. Christmas is far more what you give than what you receive. Christmas is other people's happiness. Christmas. Where will we spend Christmas?

Christian bustles around. Boxes of provisions arrive and, to our amazement, disappear into the lockers. It's astonishing how much a boat will hold. It can't be true that we're going to spend Christmas at sea. I'm so tired. What shall I do?

The boat is filling up, and settling lower in the water. Didier installs all his things: he's leaving the *Ain-Taiba.* I hear them say we'll be filled up with oil and water tomorrow. Are we leaving then? And it's December 22 today. The problem of my Christmas presents goes round and round in my tired brain. Mouchka has given me some for Christian, his brother, and Laurence. But I haven't got anything for them. If we could only stay here, we could go and sing carols, play the guitar with the others, be poor and lonely together, and it would be a real Christmas.

I ask timidly: "Surely we aren't going to leave on Christmas Eve."

"Why not? What do you want to stay in this awful, filthy, depressing harbor for? Our first Christmas at sea will be wonderful. It's a family occasion. Anyway, we've made all the arrangements. We leave tomorrow morning, as soon as we've been filled up with water."

It's still drizzling at Las Palmas, and the harbor is still rough. The boats moored alongside each other rattle and bump at regular intervals with a gloomy clanking. Gigi's white shape is silhouetted against the dark, menacing sky. I'm wearing a gray jersey outfit. Everything's gray tonight.

The wind blew all night, whistling in the rigging, and the clatter of metal and wood kept us awake. Christian got up three times to secure the halyards of the mainsail and jib, which were beating against the mast. But this morning, as if by magic, the sky is blue and the sun is shining, making everything look brighter. Ideal sailing weather.

It's now ten o'clock. We go round the harbor to say goodbye to our friends: "See you in Barbados! Merry Christmas. Happy new year."

Laurence is on deck, well wrapped up in her little nest.

The skipper notes in the log book: "Left harbor 10.10. Good northeast wind, about force 6. Gigi's working well."

And he streams the log for the first few days.

Suddenly, there's a mass of birds right in front of us.

"France! Quick—the line!"

It's a school of tuna or bonitos: the tuna chase shoals of little fish, which leap in the air in their fright and are caught by the seabirds. You only need a lure, which shines like a small fish, for the tuna to bite. In Polynesia they use a bit of gleaming mother-of-pearl, slightly curved and crescent-shaped, without a hook; the bonito takes the lure, the fisherman draws in the line with a wide sweeping movement, and the fish lands on his legs, which he's covered with a gunny sack. The fish unhooks itself of its own accord, and the fisherman casts his line again immediately. His basket is soon filled. Sharks usually join in this bloodthirsty sport; they are after the bonito. Sometimes the boat brings back a swordfish.

We use an ordinary spoon armed with a hook. It's fixed to the few yards of wire attached to the end of the nylon line so that a large fish can't bite through it. As soon as the spoon touches the water there's a tug. Christian lands a fine twelve- or fourteen-pound bonito. That's enough for us. We reel up the line, which could get tangled in the log.

I cut off some fillets straight away. We eat them raw, and I crush some to extract the juice, which Laurence thoroughly enjoys. I dice the rest into cubes to marinate in lemon juice, á la Tahitienne. The head—the best part—will make a delicious risotto for supper.

"Constant strong wind," the log for the next day says. "Impossible to run with the wind directly astern, because we veer too much to the west. On the quarter. Waves as high as the mast."

Leaning against the engine, with my baby in my arms, I admire

38

the efficient way Gigi works. Every time a wave tries to bring us to, she firmly rights the seven- or eight-ton *Alpha* with a little movement of her twenty-five-by-twelve-centimeter trimming tab. To see the tops of the waves I have to raise my head as far as I can. They're like a wall in front of me. I can't bear to think what would happen if that great mass broke over us. But, being so low, we ought to sink like a barrel and re-emerge after the deluge—provided we haven't shipped too much water. Being cautious and apprehensive by nature, I'm amazed to feel safe. It's because I have faith in our skipper, and in the *Alpha*. Metal casks aren't smashed by the sea.

It's a dramatic kind of Christmas Day. But nothing to what Bernard Moitessier must have seen rounding Cape Horn. We're all fighting against seasickness. Christian and Didier were sick last night, but it wore off. I'm still feeling the effect of the Marzine. But I can't take the smell of tobacco and Didier has to smoke his Gauloises outside. It's a good idea anyway. There's no question of opening the forehatch in this weather, and there's not much ventilation. I don't want Laurence to breathe in cigarette smoke.

Tonight the sunset is a wonderful blaze of red and mauve, making the sea violet as the twilight deepens.

Nightfall at sea is a crucial moment. Before it's dark, you must see that the boat's perfectly in order; you've had a meal; Laurence is in bed. The skipper has got to be able to find the right-sized wrench or the flashlight in the dark without a moment's hesitation.

As it grows dark, Christian scans the horizon and casts an expert eye over sea and sky. He estimates the strength of the wind, and tries to foresee as best he can what kind of weather there'll be during the next few hours.

At night there's no light and it's difficult to judge distances. If the sky is overcast the darkness is complete. It's very difficult to change a jib quickly. Even more difficult to see a seam that is tearing. Although Gigi steers perfectly the skipper feels very alone then and responsible for us all. Even asleep, with one eye he keeps a watch over the *Alpha*'s progress from his bunk. Which is why we always leave the roof open and sleep under the stars all the year round.

Underwater life becomes more alarming. Creatures become

phosphorescent. Plankton looms up in luminous green sheets. Sometimes a bluish-green shape several yards long glides round the boat like a ghost pursuing us. The silence, broken only by the creaking of the *Alpha,* makes you shiver apprehensively. You are in the middle of a black desert.

But tonight our skipper doesn't look as preoccupied as usual at this time of day. He's happy. He hasn't even asked if supper is ready. It isn't because we'll dine late tonight, at about half past eight. It's Christmas Eve.

Thanks to the *Erna,* our fare will be festive: a Cassegrain cassoulet instead of turkey. A Mont-Blanc praline mousse instead of a yule log. And as a finishing touch, a small bottle of real champagne. Unfortunately our stomachs aren't quite ready for such a rich meal. But . . .

"Christ the Savior is born. Sing, choirs . . ." Christian has just switched on the radio receiver. It's a surprise, because it's usually kept strictly for time checks; we have to save the batteries. And now, just by turning a switch, he has linked us to the rest of the world: "Ring bells . . . Silent night, holy night . . ."

We left the Canaries only two days ago, but we're already a long way off. If we wanted to go back it would take at least ten days in this weather. And a month separates us from Barbados the other way. Lost in the middle of these huge waves we're safe in the *Alpha* as we keep our first Christmas at sea. And we are filled with wonder as the tiny cabin resounds with the voices of thousands of men and women like ourselves who are singing the same carols in every language: "While shepherds watched . . . Adeste fideles . . . Oh Christmas Tree . . . Christians awake . . . Hark! The herald angels sing . . ." We've never experienced anything like it. If only all the people who are singing tonight could know how it warms us on the *Alpha* this Christmas Eve, although we're each wearing two or three sweaters, and it's 59 degrees outside—and if we meet a submerged object in the dark our hull could split open, landing us in water two or three miles deep.

Our Christmas is very frugal. Christian is the only one who gives any presents: Didier a box of cigars, Laurence a little rubber lamb, which makes a cheerful "squeak, squeak," and me a beautiful stamp album. I'm miserable at not having anything to give. And yet

40

filled with the marvelous joy of Christmas, because of this little radio receiver.

"I bring you good tidings . . ." We're so happy we can't speak. We're not listening, we're *there,* part of Christmas. We're singing with the choirs and our own voices, our whole life, rings out from the little set. Each one recalls childhood Christmases. We relive them afresh, vividly, like old men savoring for the last time the joys and disappointments of a lifetime, as if we were about to die. Tonight we are there in the stable, and Laurence is our divine child. She's asleep, but I'm sure she can feel our happiness as she lies there, that it enfolds her.

The rattling of her counting frame wakes me from a deep sleep. The emotions of the previous evening have tired me out. When I sit up I see a little face smiling at the lamb hanging above her basket.

"Merry Christmas, Laurence! Your first Christmas."

Didier's still asleep. We can make a diabolical din all around him and he still doesn't wake up. If there's an emergency we have to shake him.

It's a lovely day and Laurence feeds hungrily. When she's full she goes on sucking for the fun of it, and plays with my dark hair. I'm touched by the utter confidence she has in me, and sometimes feel afraid of disappointing her. In her mother's arms, nothing unpleasant can happen.

"Ouch!"

I screamed so loudly that Laurence was scared. She screamed too, starting to cry. I'd spilled the boiling hot chocolate Christian made all over myself. Luckily none went on Laurence. Christian scrapes a large potato to make a cold poultice. Later I'll put on some grease. If it was more serious I'd give my leg a good soaking in salt water. When on land the best thing is to cover the burn immediately with the sap of a young banana tree.

After drowning, fire is the worst danger on a boat. We take every possible precaution. We have no gasoline on board—our engine uses oil—and gas is in small cylinders. In fact, since these were filled in Las Palmas there's been a strong smell of leaking gas. The difficulty is that gas sinks to the bottom of the boat. To get rid of it you've got to extract it. If it is allowed to accumulate it will

41

explode at the smallest spark. We ought to throw the cylinders overboard and use the Primus, which burns kerosene. On checking we can't find a leak. But the smell? I open the locker under my bunk: the smell is so strong it knocks me back. Then I see a green streak, and am greatly relived to discover what has happened: when we had the cylinders refilled we disconnected the pipe that joins the cylinder to the stove. The pipe is covered with a thick green liquid that makes the gas smell strongly if it is escaping. While the pipe was on the sink the liquid ran over the draining board and dripped into my locker. So there's no leak. After this scare we seriously consider getting a good Primus with two burners. But they're expensive.

I've got used to the large waves, but I limit my excursions on deck as much as possible, only going out when it's essential, to put the washing out for instance.

"Christian! The line's taut!"

But he's already there. The system he's set up in the cabin, which originally consisted of a line attached to the big toe of his left foot, has dislodged his pillow. He likes to know at once if a fish bites so that a bigger one won't come and snap it up—with the spoon. We've already lost three in this way. Didier and he haul in the line, winding it around a bit of board as they go along so that it won't get tangled.

A fine dorado weighing almost twenty pounds struggles on the deck, beating its great tail, while Laurence watches with a mixture of fear and delight. Its colors fade quickly: its blue and gold back changes to a luminous green and then to a dull gray. Its sulfur-yellow belly rapidly becomes a dirty white. Its skin was perfectly smooth only a minute ago, and now it's rough, showing each scale.

We sprinkle the fish with lemon juice and it makes a fine feast. I make an incision at the base of the head and around the gills, and the skin comes away easily. We fall on the deliciously fresh raw flesh like savages.

I've got a pain. It's very localized, up by my appendix. A burning sensation, which comes and goes. It must be a slight inflammation of the ovary, which the doctor said I had when I was expecting Laurence. But it gets worse and worse. Then stops. It must be my ovary. But it's hurting again. . . .

My right side hurts, still in the same place. It's not getting any worse. It must be my ovary. I hope it is. I hope—but supposing it isn't? If it's . . . Remember that American who left Panama for Polynesia with his wife. They were alone on a lovely sloop with a white plastic hull. A fortnight later the American came back alone: his wife had had a burst appendix.

No. It's not possible. Anyway we've got antibiotics and syringes; three syringes and four needles. Christian's never done an injection but he can learn. You can do anything if you have to. I can last out for ten days or so. But we're at least three weeks from the nearest hospital. If I can only last a fortnight.

Laurence will be motherless. Christian couldn't go on alone with her. Who would he get to look after her? She'd be put in a home. It's too awful. My darling little daughter put in a home. How would she be brought up, and where? No, it's not possible. I can't have appendicitis. The pain's still there, coming and going.

It must be my ovary. It must be, otherwise the pain would get worse. I'd be in agony and couldn't bend my leg up to my stomach. It *must* be my ovary. I haven't done anything to deserve that. Besides, the pain's wearing off, not getting worse. I'm terribly hot.

I creep into Christian's bed and he smiles.

"Christian, do you think it would be possible to go back to Las Palmas?"

"It would take at least a fortnight. It's out of the question in this weather. It wouldn't be any quicker than going to Barbados. But what's up?"

"Nothing. It's silly. I had a bit of a pain."

"Where?"

"You know, my ovary, I think. I thought it might be appendicitis."

"Don't be silly. You know how it is at sea—the instinct to survive. Divine providence perhaps. People are never really ill. It's impossible."

"Maybe."

To live with the thought of death, feel as if each moment were the last. Perhaps it would help us to waste less time in trivialities, to live up to our aspirations, devote ourselves to them more fully.

4

Flying Fish in the Atlantic

It seems it's very fashionable to cross the Atlantic these days, but the voyage remains a major undertaking. On a boat the size of the *Alpha* it takes at least twenty-eight days to get from the Canaries to the West Indies. You must have an extra month's supply of food and water in case the voyage should take longer. Menus have to be worked out carefully, and it must be borne in mind that people have large appetites at sea. You must have fresh foodstuffs that will last well, a reserve supply of vitamin pills, and plenty of water.

We bought twenty pounds of green bananas at Las Palmas. We've been at sea six days and there's only one apiece left. Bananas take up a lot of room and are deceptively bulky. As they all ripen at the same time even if each is carefully wrapped in newspaper, you are forced to eat them quickly. It's very difficult to find bunches of bananas in the markets that are green enough. We'll try to do better in the Antilles, so that they last longer.

The bread is beginning to go moldy today. Here, too, in spite of "baker's" packs, with treated paper and plastic bags, all the bread begins to get moldy at the same time, possibly because there are four of us living in a very small space, making the atmosphere hot and damp. Cabbages, lemons, onions, and potatoes last well, the cabbages about two weeks and the rest at least a month, provided you inspect them regularly and take out any that are going bad. If we had a freezer, or even a refrigerator, we could of course store tomatoes, peppers, and cucumbers. Luckily we catch at least one dorado a day. We'll have plenty of fresh fish all the way to Tahiti.

We carry 150 gallons of water: three quarts a day per person for two months. Laurence has her own special allocation—forty gallons provided by Evian. I give her some between each feeding, so that she doesn't get dehydrated. She also has a two-month supply of canned milk, in case I can't feed her.

You must also be sure you have enough fuel to cook with. A German who was sailing alone from Los Angeles to Tahiti had carefully installed two cylinders of gas on deck. He didn't notice or smell the gas escaping and found himself with a few cans of food and nothing else but uncooked rice and flour. After a few spectacular attempts to obtain heat by burning diesel oil, he had to eat rice soaked in cold water for twenty-five days.

A lucky break. The wind has died down, the weather continues fine, and this respite gives me renewed energy. I sing as I work, from morning till night. I've watched Laurence playing for an hour: she does all sorts of things with three rings on a chain. It makes me laugh when her little hand, still not able to judge distances properly, goes out toward something and falls on thin air. Even when she's alone she babbles away, smiling to herself, which makes me feel she must be happy.

It's a funny idea having an engine on a small boat in mid-ocean. Or not so funny. I have spent over an hour cleaning up splashes of thick, inky-black oil from the sump. Christian ran the engine for an hour this morning: what a din. Laurence hated it. The hand starter wouldn't work, and the skipper spent two hours greasing it everywhere. And the sump of the crankcase is indescribable, with the

45

rocking of the boat at sea. There is oil everywhere, on the varnished woodwork, the mattresses, a toy, in the galley. I'll go on finding spots of oil in various places for at least a week, and they spread and never wash out.

The automatic pilot has revolutionized pleasure cruising, utterly transforming life on board during a long voyage.

I remember the watches we used to take on the *Carmellia.* Some people love spending hours peering at a compass on a starless night, but I don't. There is, of course, the fantastic beauty of starlit skies, of balmy nights, the sunrise—gorgeous storms too; but when they happen everyone is on deck and there's no time to think. You can enjoy it all just as much with an automatic pilot. All you have to do is go up on deck at the right moment. On the *Alpha,* if there's exceptionally bad weather, we are fresh and rested when we take the tiller, thanks to Gigi. Without her, life on board with a baby would be far too exhausting. Even with her, the days seem far too short to me. I only get about half an hour a day for reading.

It's the first time I've seen Christian put on his safety harness to go on deck. The swell is so heavy that it is like being under water. Everything is lashed down securely and we are sandwiched between the waves above and the ocean below. We think of the cosmonauts bravely flying in their capsules. Our steel hull is very reassuring.

Navigation poses a problem. It's very difficult to take readings from the sextant in this weather. You need two hands and you can't keep your balance without holding on. Christian can only estimate roughly, using the sun when it makes a brief appearance—if the *Alpha* happens to be on the crest of a wave. And is it because of the bad weather that we can't hear Lisbon any longer? We'll have to find another station on our old receiver.

Those who talk of the great empty, silent stretches of the ocean should be on the *Alpha* tonight. What with the noise of the waves, the crash of the hull on the water, the grinding of the mast, the screeching of the wind in the rigging, and a tin can that is rolling about and can't be found, there is enough noise to wake the dead.

Every day Christian notes that we have caught the largest dorado since we left—which is true. Today it's almost twenty-four

46

pounds. There's a simple explanation: the same school of dorados has been following us all the time and they're getting bigger and bigger. We can recognize one of them because we cut it on the back with a harpoon ten days ago. That one will never take a bite at the spoon. But the school will stay with us as far as Barbados. Sometimes we find in one of their stomachs a can lid that we've thrown into the sea. Yesterday—New Year's Day—we had our fish with mayonnaise, a present from the *Erna*. We try to eat some raw vegetables every day, making a first course for three people with a grated carrot, two cabbage leaves, two onions, six rounds of cucumber. We keep the salads small so that we can have them for as long as possible. Toward the end of the crossing we'll be eating raw onion with salt and raw potato dressed with oil and vinegar. Everything tastes good at sea—but I never get enough, as I'm feeding Laurence.

"The water's much warmer," announces the skipper, who has just had to go for a swim to rebolt Gigi, who is getting much too independent again. With the wind blowing this way and that, lurching and rocking, she has struggled on valiantly hour after hour, but since Las Palmas the sea and the wind have given her no rest. Rudely buffeted, she has gradually worked loose, rattling more and more, and the skipper felt more and more guilty about her. It's not much fun putting screws in in the water when the boat's moving. Thanks to the harness we needn't heave to. Which would be very unpleasant in this weather.

"Guess what I found on deck this morning? Some exocoetus."

I had difficulty remembering what these flying fish were called. They have highly developed fins that enable them to escape from the hungry dorados. They glide over the water for hundreds of feet. We timed one, which flew for over three minutes: each time it wanted to come down it saw a dorado. Fear really did lend it wings. Exocoetus can go at a speed of up to twenty-five miles an hour. They are delicious to eat, cooked or raw. Their flesh is as tender as a sardine's, but less oily.

The sail shines in the moonlight; they are attracted by it, and crash into the jib, falling on the deck. As we are low in the water, most of them manage to get back into the sea. But there are five left, so we can have raw fish with our porridge, for our first breadless breakfast. It's encouraging, because flying fish are a sign that we are now in the trade-wind zone. In a day or two the sea will be much warmer and the sun burning hot. We'll be able to go naked. Washing will be much pleasanter too. We have a shower every day, which consists of scrubbing ourselves with a brush and throwing several buckets of water over ourselves, including our hair. It makes our skin glow and we feel very fit. Laurence has a salt-water bath too, with water warmed in the sun.

"A month in this little capsule in the middle of the ocean is a testing time," the skipper writes; *"hard on the nerves and sometimes a trial of physical endurance. You can't undertake the venture lightly. The nervous strain is immense. Having to get along with people for weeks on end, in a small space with no means of getting away, even for a minute. People's faults become extraordinarily exaggerated."*

"If you want a crew, marry it," one navigator has said.

But even for a married couple it's a trying time. It's an abnormal situation. You've soon exhausted your partner's possibilities, or feel as though you have. You think you know them absolutely. And it is then, when you think you've said everything, that it's vital to have something more to say to each other. Otherwise it is fatal.

A year at sea, cooped up with your husband for twenty-four hours out of twenty-four is the equivalent of twenty years of married life. The unfortunate thing is that at the end of the year you are not forty: you haven't the experience, or maturity, or forbearance to be able to cope with someone whom you know so completely. You are still vulnerable. So you get divorced, or realize that you do really love each other.

It is worse with three. Although Didier is our brother and a discreet and pleasant crewmate, he is still there all the time, sharing our marriage. If you swear at your husband in private it's unimportant. But in front of someone else it matters. One reacts more violently out of wounded pride, and quarrels become blown-up because subconsciously neither of you wants to lose face. In a habitable space of fifteen square feet I can't fling myself into Christian's arms after a fight. Even if I did, both the third person—who is supposed not to have noticed anything—and Christian would be embarrassed. So feelings that might still be salvaged at the time of

48

the explosion are slowly forgotten, freeze, and die.

We don't quite realize what is happening, and neither of us can understand the growing gulf between us. We no longer communicate, but go off at a tangent. What can we do about it?

But happiness is there, it exists, if only we could find it. The ocean is like a vast symphony, an orchestra made up of a multitude of infinitely varied colors, of living shapes, of spray on your face, of sunrises and sunsets, which all move to the rhythm of the wind. This powerful music, which has been a part of me from the moment I was born, which is my life itself, throbs and roars in my head. The music of the sea fills me; I drown in it. I feel that my body can no longer contain it, that I will explode; a great feeling of power surges through me, and a consciousness of this beauty in which I am plunged, which I breathe in, which takes my breath away. This beauty that catches at my throat, at my guts, that makes me want to shout at the top of my voice. That makes me want to cry.

What immense happiness: life eternally renewed before our very eyes, in all the perfection of nature. A wave, a bird, a fish are never ordinary, they always have that delicate beauty that corresponds to the aspirations of the soul—the *anima* aspiring to all that it is not. All the most powerful, all the most subtle human characteristics are there in profusion in these calm or turbulent waters.

The sea is a school that teaches integrity, courage, and patience. One learns to think things through; to discover the true value of things, the real meaning of the word *life,* which is the opposite of death. The ocean is a marvelous teacher. You can't escape her laws, her demands. She never forgives. After an experience like this, you understand how far civilization has come, how many thousands of years of work and research have gone into the discovery of electric light, radar, cars, the luxurious and comfortable houses of our so-called consumer society. And you then consume these things with pleasure and great gratitude for the millions of people who have made the path of progress possible for us.

Happiness at sea. The sea brings us face to face with ourselves. There are no neighbors, no others to refer to, no one to imitate, or to criticize you. Everything you do is either vitally necessary or fulfills a profound wish. My behavior is no longer conditioned by society. I become aware of my personality, discover the meaning of sincerity—being frank with oneself. Life is reduced to essentials at sea and it is impossible or dangerous to encumber oneself with false reasons, false motivations. Life is so short: we mustn't waste the time given us. At sea one must always do the right thing at the right moment. The life of a crewmate or even of the whole boat could be at stake. You finish up having the same attitude toward all your actions, or if you don't, it is better not to go to sea.

We're now comfortably in the trade winds. The weather is perfect: the wind moderate, the sea even. It's 97 degrees in the saloon. The forecastle hatch is permanently open and the *Alpha* is beautifully airy. We all, including Laurence, wear swimsuits all day long.

Since we reached the trade winds and the bad weather left us, the men's favorite pastime is fishing. Didier tells us about the fantastic catches he made in the West Indies last year, and Christian plays around making triple hooks. Didier fishes for the fun of it; he loves the sport, beating his own record.

We don't like killing creatures that love life as much as we do. So, to compromise, the skipper decides that we'll dry any fish left over to eat on the days when we don't catch anything.

It's a good idea, but we don't know the right method. In Tahiti there is so much fish all the year round that no one bothers to keep it. For me, dried or salted fish or meat conjures up the tough existence of Arctic fishermen, or the poverty of underdeveloped countries. We haven't quite reached that point. Christian is thinking about the delicious smoked kippers you get in Equiheen where the Guillains had property.

"You have to cut very thin fillets, like this." And he hangs them in the rigging. The sun is our refrigerator, he notes. If a dorado is too big, we cut off some to eat and the fillets dry in the rigging, where they hang nicely.

The next day, longing to try them, he takes some down for me to grill. He eats a mouthful raw on the way. They crackle in the pan and smell delicious. We attack our plates.

"Delicious," Christian says.

"Famous," agrees Didier.

"They're a bit strong," I say timidly.

"That doesn't matter," replies Christian. "Bonitos get a bit strong when they're kept too long, but they're still all right."

Suddenly he goes very red. "It's awfully hot!"

His chest, back, and arms are covered with red marks, which turn yellow and then violet. Then the patches start swelling up.

At the same moment Didier gets up to get some air: "It's so hot. Good heavens, Guillian, have you seen your back and chest and arms?"

And we all shriek together: "The fish!"

"Try and make yourself sick, quickly."

It sounds easy, on a boat at sea, but it's not. We all three stand in the cockpit with fingers down our throats, but it's no good. I fill a mug with sea water and add two tablespoonfuls of salt. Drink it down, feeling sick—and nothing happens. Blast. If you're not feeling seasick, it's incredibly difficult to vomit. We have to laugh at our ridiculous plight. We retch and swallow mug after mugful, and at last, by sheer will power, achieve it.

Then we all stuff ourselves with charcoal and anything in the medicine chest that can be used for food poisoning. Didier and Christian are all right, but I don't know if it will have affected my milk. I consult Dr. Spock and Laurence Pernoud, who are not very helpful. To be on the safe side, I give Laurence bottled milk for forty-eight hours.

She takes the bottle well, but makes a funny face, as if she were mystified. She's lost her usual liveliness, and doesn't chatter to me any more. "Avoid abrupt weaning," my book says. I can't bear it. But the inevitable happens: my breasts swell, my milk nearly stops. For two long days I keep Laurence beside me in the bunk and let her feed as much as she can whenever she likes. I don't give her any milk in a bottle but only Evian water. If she wants to live she must suck. On the third day my milk slowly comes back, and we've won. We've succeeded so well in fact that she can breast feed until she's thirteen months old. Her sparkle returns; she smiles and babbles again. Everything's all right.

In Barbados we learn that one must cut the fillets very fine, salt them before drying them, and keep them away from the spray. It's particularly important not to leave them out at night. And they told us dorados keep very badly.

51

Meanwhile we're off fish for the rest of the trip. We were lucky to have a reaction at once, as soon as it reached our stomachs. We could all have died of food poisoning.

So we go back to the cans. It isn't really enough for us while we're at sea. Mealtimes become traumatic. It's difficult to write about this—people don't usually mention this kind of detail because it is not very nice. It's something that happens at sea; it stops as soon as we sight land.

I hate the sharing out at mealtimes, but can't bear to miss it. From the way he rushes up, Didier obviously feels the same. Christian is the central figure in the drama: the skipper divides up the rations. We don't dole out everything: rice, haricot beans, chickpeas, are no problem. But sardines are more difficult. There's seldom the right number to be divided by three, and when there is, they're not the same size. You have to assess them, cut them up carefully and fairly, mentally weighing them. Each of us knows at once, without saying a word or making a movement, which bit he wants. And, as with small children, even if you do happen to get the share you've chosen, other people's plates look more desirable. Naturally this all takes place in complete silence. No one dares mention it; everyone is secretly rather ashamed, but twice a day the same emotions can be seen all too clearly for a minute or two on each face. As it's the skipper who divides the portions, he is the target for our suspicions. We both feel that he's doing better than we. We're wrong of course; he isn't.

At sea, eating is of course vital, but it's also an important distraction. You've very hungry; you think about food all the time, and imagine what you might be eating on land at that moment. You spend hours looking at beautiful color photographs of roasts, chicken, cakes, crème Chantilly, pêches Melba. You read recipes, and simple words such as "butter" or vanilla send you into a trance. On land we hardly ever think about food. We spend as little time as possible in the kitchen and aren't at all greedy. And then as soon as we're at sea we commit the sin of envy every day, coveting our neighbor's share. As you can't question the skipper's orders, even if they have nothing to do with the running of the boat, you repress your feelings and hate the others for a fraction of a second, then feel ashamed because it's so absurd. It's very easy to unload your own sins onto other people. For a few seconds, Christian becomes the scapegoat.

Didier is splicing the mainsheet, getting a few last puffs from the fag end of a damp cigarette, which he has clumsily rolled himself. On the automatic pilot, the *Alpha* is slipping along at four or five knots toward Barbados. It's marvelous weather. The swell is lively without being rough, the sky a tropical blue. This isn't the clear hot blue of Provence, but a subdued blue, veiled with streaks of white cloud from the mists which rise from the sea in the heat. The sails and deck are brilliantly, blindingly white.

Christian is stretched out on his bunk on the starboard side. He suddenly looks at his watch, at the compass, at Gigi, at the sail. He seizes the sextant, gives a pencil and paper to Didier, who drops his splice and takes his brother's watch to use a chronometer.

"Wow," says Christian, "it's ten minutes to midday."

Balancing on his legs, he squints behind the sextant to estimate the height of the sun. Didier jots down at regular intervals: 317° 24'4" at 9h0m45s; 317°18'2" at 9h09m35s. In the cockpit the bath thermometer is floating in a yellow bucket: 97 degrees Fahrenheit.

The *Alpha* will reach the Antilles in a few days.

5

Land

Laurence has just had her morning bath. I'm feeding her on the foredeck, leaning against the pulpit. The bowsprit rises rhythmically; the hull is covered with a coat of green weed, which slows us up. The hull and deck are steel, so there are streaks of yellow rust running across the paintwork, but we don't remove them. In a few days' time they will be the signs by which the *Alpha,* our seabird, can be distinguished from the swarm of Sunday yachts and glossy charter boats that crowd the little harbors in the Grenadines. With the wind astern, we're sailing under the mainsail and the jib on a small spar. The motion is smooth and not at all tiring. The sun is directly overhead and I shade Laurence with my body. We set out thirty days ago. I think Pierre and Catherine took thirty-one days in the *Vencia,* so we should arrive tomorrow. But with so little wind . . .

My baby is asleep and the pressure cooker is whistling. It's rather difficult crossing the deck with a baby in your arms. Christian is in the saloon, spreading on the table one of the many charts given to us by the *Saint-Briac.* The sextant has been carefully put back in its padded box. A book of HO 214 tables and the *Nautical Almanac* are on the seat. He is fixing our position.

While I'm putting Laurence gently back in her basket, where she lies comfortably spread-eagled, Didier turns off the stove. He opens the two-gallon pan, which is two-thirds full of rice and rounds of smoked sausage, and looks delighted as the steam hits him in the face.

Finally Christian looks up with a satisfied smile.

"How far?" we both ask together.

"Only 175 miles."

We have been saying "only" ever since we reached the half-way mark between the Canaries and the Antilles. This has replaced the "already" of the first few days, but will be followed by an exasperated "more" if we don't get there tomorrow.

While I dish up, Christian puts away the chart with its beautifully drawn curve of the *Alpha's* course. He hangs the dividers neatly on the bulkhead, with the pencil, parallel ruler, and rubber.

Since midday each of us has been watching the dark line on the horizon, which never seems to get any bigger, because there's so little wind. Christian is experiencing the pleasure of a skipper who has succeeded in steering his boat toward a minute speck in the ocean. You can cross the Atlantic on a raft and find land on the other side, but it's extremely satisfying when you're only in your twenties to decide a month in advance on the exact point where you will land, and steer your own yacht there.

He writes: *"What a marvelous feeling to be on the other side of the Atlantic on my own boat! I really feel that I've achieved what I set out to do. There's a lot to do on board, but the sun is shining, the sea is blue, and soon there'll be white sands and a peaceful lagoon, and all our life in front of us."*

We get out razors and makeup box and I cut my two pirates'

hair. We have to change from the hirsute savages we've become into well-groomed, elegant creatures. We represent France, since the *Alpha* is legally a bit of our country that has traveled across the world. We must do our best to look good.

We can sense that land is near. There's a warm haze of mist round us. It's 9 P.M. We sit under the waning moon and wait—we're not at all sleepy.

The old lantern swings gently on the backstay. We haven't seen another boat for thirty days, but there's a greater risk here. A faint light dances over the water. Then there's the sputter of an engine. It's very difficult to judge distances in the dark. A boat seems to be coming toward us. Possibly attracted by our light? It suddenly appears less than a cable length away, coming straight across our bows. It must have seen us. There is only a light wind, and we're hove to, which makes it difficult to maneuver. Christian shines the flashlight on the sail, and signals. The boat keeps its course. I am shaking with fear but Christian is calm and ready to start up the engine if necessary. We have a hand starter, because other people's experience has shown us how many yachts have run aground on a reef because the battery was run down. And also the skipper gives our little diesel a trial run every week. At the end of a few minutes, which seem like hours, the old tub passes within a few yards of the bowsprit, without veering an inch off course to avoid us. Christian whistles loudly as the *Alpha* rocks violently in the wake of the fishing boat. They probably didn't even see us. I shudder to think that we could have been peacefully asleep, counting on Gigi and our light to protect us. To be so close to disaster only a few hours from land.

Large boats generally see our steel hull on their radar screens. Eventually they will sweep the sea with their powerful searchlights to locate us. This had happened to us in the Mediterranean once or twice. But on the main Atlantic and Pacific lines the radar isn't permanently switched on. A yacht is small in comparison with the height of the waves and the cargo ships go very fast. It sometimes happens that a yacht isn't spotted in time, and it's almost impossible to survive if the boat is cut in two. Christian and Didier will take watches tonight. To cheer himself up at the beginning of his, Didier switches on the radio receiver and puts on the earphones. He rocks

56

to the music and it looks very funny when you can't hear anything yourself. I take a turn and begin moving to a jerky rhythm. It's marvelous to be in touch with people again: we've been cut off for thirty days. When you've been knocking around in a steel capsule and haven't seen land for a month, you've almost forgotten what it's like. We feel as though our life on shore was in another world, like a dream. But when a real island rises from the ocean in the brilliant dawn light of the Tropics, with real trees, real sand, real houses, we feel as if we could dance over the waves to reach it. It's miraculous. At last we're here.

The skipper stands proudly at the helm. He must make a smooth approach, with no mistakes. We execute a slalom between the boats in the bay, looking for yachts we know, or French yachts, or just to say we're here.

"Where do you come from?"

"From France."

"Hi! Paris!"

Barbados used to be English.

A man comes up to us in a little dinghy with an outboard motor: "You're French?"

"Yes, are you?"

"Yes, I've been here a few days. Come and moor alongside the *Vap*. Do you need anything?"

"A little sugar if you can spare it," says Christian, who has hated having his tea without it.

"A cigarette," Didier adds, his eyes lighting up.

Our quarantine flag is hoisted with the courtesy flag. The authorities arrive and are very pleasant, and the formalities are soon over. At last we can land.

We weigh anchor at once and go on to Bridgetown harbor, where huge schooners are moored, some of which, with no engines, trade from island to island. Everything in this old English colonial town is ochre, red, blue, and black.

It feels strange to be on land. You don't roll but you feel weightless, as if you're going to take off and fly. I long to run and stretch my legs. At sea your whole body is perpetually in motion, but making contracted movements, not stretching. No comparison with a good walk on dry land.

The streets are full of bustle. The population is pure-bred Africa, with few half-castes. There is a mixture of puritanism and smiling, slightly submissive expansiveness, which is touching.

It seems to be the cool season—luckily—as it's 95 degrees in the shade. Woolen suits, stockings, and coats are *de rigueur.* Even the babies can hardly see out of their layers of pink wool.

"She'll catch cold," they say, pointing at Laurence, who's only wearing a thin cotton smock.

We spend three hours in the grilling sun buying provisions. It's marvelous to be able to get tomatoes, fresh meat, bananas, mangoes, and a papaya. Didier and Christian carry the supplies in loads of a dozen kilos.

Near the market, old women converge on us from all sides: "Let me have your pretty baby, let me hold her." And they smile broadly, showing white teeth. I have to ward off their caresses tactfully. But how kind they are. During the whole week I never once carry a heavy load back to the boat. One of them always comes up to take my bag of shopping as far as the quay, from sheer kindness of heart. I have never known this happen anywhere else.

Faint with hunger, we leave the harbor to go and drop anchor near the *Vap* in Carlisle Bay. We are sixty yards from the beach.

We eat on deck for a change, under an improvised awning, while Pierre, the skipper of the *Vap,* tells us about his voyage. His boat is a motor-sailer, to which he has devoted all his time for months. He treats her as if she were a jewel. She seems like a floating palace to us. An after cabin, with the large double berth of our dreams, partitioned off, a saloon with all the woodwork varnished—it is all quite perfect, roomy, electric, electronic, automatic. But what a constant worry it must be. It would be sheer slavery, especially with a wooden hull: one has to beware of worms in warm seas.

The turquoise bay is so clear that you can see a spoon twenty feet down. On the white sand palm trees bend their graceful fronds to the limpid water. The sky above is a meltingly soft blue.

It's hard to describe: words and photographs can't do it justice, any more than you can describe the blue mists that spread over Paris at nightfall in the autumn. All this light, these colors are our private world today, while some people are spending their day on

58

the subway. All we need to do to go on the beach is slip into the water. I must hitch a lift to the shore to take the two large sailbags bursting with dirty clothes, and my three-month-old baby, who is beginning to crawl everywhere on all fours.

Dong. Dong. Dong! I haven't heard a clock strike for months. Sitting on our bunk I quietly lift up the forehatch and put my head out to hear better. Christian is fast asleep beside me.

Dong. Dong. Dong! Twelve strokes. It is midnight.

The moon bathes the sleeping coconut palms in its golden light. A scarcely perceptible swell rocks the hundred-odd boats gently. I can hear the distant suck of the surf on the shore, and the cheerful clanking of rigging.

In a few days all the boats from the Canaries will be here: the *Mamari,* the *Anahita,* the *Rhâ* and possibly the *Ain-Taiba.*

The golden moon.

When I was seven we lived at Auae, by the sea, four miles from Papeete. I loved my silent encounters with the moon and stars. I felt as if the moon were enveloping me, absorbing me. There were hardly any houses and very few cars. You could lie in the middle of the road under the great arch of the balsam trees. There was no sound except for the lapping of the sea, and my father and I would stand there side by side, spellbound. I held tightly to his hand for reassurance. I felt as though I were going to be sucked up into those myriad worlds which shone above us, all round us. Their reflections made white zebra stripes across the dark water. I felt so small, so small. "Look, there's a shooting star, a star which has burst. It could be a meteor. A few years ago a meteor fell over there, between Mooréa and Tahiti, and it caused a tidal wave."

Six o'clock in the cockpit. Laurence's first feeding. The sun, just coming over the horizon, is burning hot. The rude awakening of the Tropics—not at all like the slow progression of cold mornings that prolong the sleepiness of the night. As soon as the cock crows, there is an explosion of warm life. Birds squawk. The first tenders streak across the bay, making a great din. The tide has turned, the sea is higher and the breakers thunder on the deserted beach. A light breeze ripples through the coconut palms with a gentle rustling. In the Tropics it is as if everything is rushing madly onward, determined to live intensely, like those rose trees from Europe that flower incessantly for two years and then die exhausted.

Smells mingle with the sounds. The spicy smell of the water, the delicious aroma of toast and coffee and bacon and eggs, which are being prepared all round us, the heavy scent of tropical flowers —they all flood over the *Alpha* with the torrid heat, which suddenly engulfs the closed saloon.

The water is limpid: a fairly strong current drains the bay into the open sea. Here and there a blond bearded head or a large pair of blue eyes under a tousled dark mop emerges from a neighboring hatch. A little farther off a slender dark-haired girl is contemplating a morning swim. Friendly greetings are exchanged in every language, the most common expression being the casual American "Hi!"

Everyone helps newcomers spontaneously. In each port this helps you avoid unnecessary trouble: thanks to those who arrived before you, you will know the mood of the inhabitants and of the authorities. He will know where to do your washing and what it will cost; where you can get sails mended or an engine repaired. He can tell you that European vegetables are in short supply here, but that meat is extremely cheap, whether fillet steak or shin of beef or stewing beef; they hack off hunks of frozen meat with a saw. Whoever he may be, your "neighbor" knows everything you in turn will hand on to the next arrivals. Sometimes he has news of yachts we know, and if he has met any French people, he tells us their movements. The world of the ocean-going sailor is very small.

Three masks, three snorkel, three pairs of flippers, two weighted belts, a wet suit and two Tahitian harpoon guns lie in a heap on the deck. The two guns are made of *purau* wood and float beautifully. They are equipped with very long, fine arrows. Christian de-rusts the points, checks them, mends a barb or a slide. He changes the worn nylon that attaches the arrow to the gun. I prepare the *tui:* lengths of rope to string the fish on. One end has a float, so that it won't get caught on the coral reefs. The other end has a metal bar five inches long, to attach to the fisherman's belt. You make a *tui* several yards long so that your catch will follow you

60

at an appropriate distance. If a shark is attracted by the blood, and attacks this easy prey, he has very little chance of carrying off one of my dear skipper's legs by mistake. Christian covers himself with coconut oil from head to foot, as a protection against the cold if they fish for a long time. Didier, who is never roused from his bunk however much racket we make, leaps up at the familiar grating of the guns on the deck. The skipper is in the water. Without losing an instant the fishing fiend gulps down a bowl of porridge, pulls on his wet suit and dives in. I follow.

I glide voluptuously in the clear, warm water, in a state of weightlessness. It's as if my almost naked body were back in my mother's womb. Perfectly relaxed and happy. From the smiles we exchange, enlarged and exaggerated by our masks, I can tell that the others feel the same. The noise from on land no longer reaches us. I can hear a dull, diffused hum, composed of high-pitched vibrations: intense underwater life or the sound of one's own body? It is all the same. Here and there silver scad swim past in pairs. There are not many clumps of coral. We are making for a wreck we spotted yesterday.

The slowness and fluidity of our movements in the water, the soft-focus effect all around us make our bodies seem smooth and regular, almost perfectly shaped. It's a strange world, where one's idea of distances is confused and objects look bigger, and yet insubstantial.

The mossy hulk of a boat is silhouetted darkly against the white sand. Little blue, red, black or bright yellow fish fix us with their round, shining eyes. They approach in waves, and in beautiful broken formations. The underwater pursuit begins. The dry sound of a loosed arrow rouses me from my dreamy state. I suddenly feel terribly guilty: Laurence is alone on board and she's awake. I signal to Christian. There's no risk of Laurence's falling overboard, or burning or electrocuting herself. She can't suffocate or cut herself. But an atavistic "you never know" relegates me to the ranks of home-bound mothers.

I'm on board the *Alpha* in two minutes flat. My little deckhand is babbling on the saloon floor. I stand in the cockpit, ready to hitch a lift ashore with my two heavy sailbags of dirty clothes. The colors are very vivid in the brilliant sunlight. As vivid as beautiful black skin dressed in red, green, or yellow—the colors of the island vegetation. The lagoon, the coconut palms, the tropical sun remind me of what Tahiti was like with Christian *before Laurence came.*

Sometimes when we got cold, we would lie in the burning sun on the white sand. Where possible we chose deserted islands so we could go naked. I found it very difficult to abandon the few inches of material that were the legacy of my upbringing. Although there was no one for miles around I felt a thousand invisible eyes staring reprovingly at me, like the eye of Cain's tomb. I had never looked at myself naked in a mirror, and suddenly felt very embarrassed by my own appearance. Always fully clad, I had lost contact with my body, and behaved almost as if I didn't have one. I am not the only person to feel like this, and if everyone had the chance to live on a desert island for a while with his partner, many marital problems would solve themselves of their own accord.

Nakedness puts us in our place. It engenders humility. We poor humans, who have no fleece or shell to protect us from the cold or blows, become aware of age-old complexes which cut us off from the one we love. In a marriage there must be complete physical harmony. And for this you must first of all be in harmony with yourself, be at peace, at ease with yourself, or in other words, love your own body. To do this you have to cultivate it, as one does one's mind. You must swim, walk, climb, run, roll in the sand. The covering must be worthy of the mind inside it. Beauty, for us, is precisely this exact balance between mind and body, between the development of the body and the spirit. Nothing to do with copying glossy magazine photographs. From this direct and total union with nature stems a kind of purity, a state of grace.

One of the things I liked best, after fishing and sunbathing, was seeing Christian climb a coconut palm. You have to climb sixty feet up a vertical trunk so rough it could flay you alive, and twenty-five or thirty inches in diameter, with only your hands and feet to help you. I was proud of my dear savage.

Happiness at sea. We could feel it coming closer. The boat was for us above all a way of getting back to our roots. We loved the sea, the wind, the hot sands and adventure. We longed for lagoons, greenness, rocks, waterfalls, and real people—people who live their own lives.

62

The purr of a little outboard motor approaching: a swoosh as the boat turns; the light scrape of an oar against the hull of the *Alpha* —ouch, the paint. It is Rick come to fetch me. With his spluttering little engine, he carries four hundred pounds safely ashore. What a luxury. One, two, three, a seventh wave; we accelerate—as long as it doesn't stall. I haven't too much confidence in the machine— but we're over the surf. We pull the dinghy up the beach and I put Laurence in the shade. Luckily the yacht club is under the trees.

Crouching on the slab of concrete, I soap and scrub for hours. We made so many clothes dirty between Saint-Tropez and Casablanca, when it was cold and stormy. While I am bending over these clothes Laurence is judiciously setting out to discover the world. For the first time since she was two weeks old, she is on dry land, on something that doesn't move. She jumps around on her red-and-white *pareo* (sarong) in little leaps like a rabbit. The sand is shiny and blindingly white. Such fascinating powder—rough and yet velvety soft—when you're only three months old. Our "cabin boy" pounces forward and comes back to the *pareo,* over and over again, until she falls headlong into the sand. Her face is a picture.

Many-colored fish hang on a spit in the cockpit. My two Guillains are disappointed that they've only caught such small fish: they are only ten to fifteen inches long, my favorite size because it means there are a lot of heads to eat. Fish heads are so delicious.

While I clean and scale them Christian cooks some rice and in less than fifteen minutes the meal is ready. For dessert we have a papaya and some guavas. To think that my mother could never make me swallow an ounce of papaya and now I'm eating them whole. It's because you miss fruit so much at sea. But it's very difficult to pick a good one. The perfect time to eat them is when they drop off the tree of their own accord when you touch them. They can be revolting or delicious. Some varieties are floury or very dry, others sweet and juicy. We like them with honey or lemon —or both together, which is how I give Laurence hers. Papayas and guavas have more vitamins than any other tropical fruits. They are rich in pectin, and have the same regulative effect as apples: they are good for diarrhea. They are also rich in carotene, and a good substitute for carrots, which are scarce and expensive in many sunny islands. Their black seeds are supposed to have all sorts of properties. My grandmother had a liver cure which consisted of swallowing nine papaya pips every morning for nine days. And the leaves of the guava have a spectacular coagulant effect: to stop a cut from bleeding you crush some leaves in your hand and put them on the wound. This should only be done if no other medical aid is at hand —as Dr. Spock would say.

It is difficult to thumb a lift sometimes when there are no boats. This happens in the afternoon when the yachtsmen, whether they are lucky enough to have an engine or not, take a well-earned siesta after a good meal at the Hilton or with friends. How to get ashore with Laurence without a dinghy?

Aunt Marinou's bath!

Four rolls of inflatable tube—it should float. As the bottom is just a sheet of plastic, Laurence will make a keel for it and it should be pretty stable if she stays lying down. Christian puts on his flippers and waits in the water. I suddenly remember how tiny the bath is, seventeen by forty inches. And there are six hundred feet to go, and the breakers. I have nightmare memories of waves when I was small. I turned over and over as if I were in a tumbler dryer, hitting the sand or shingle with my head, my feet, with my head again— and I thought it would never end. Finally I was thrown violently onto the beach and lay there dazed on the shingle. When I got up I was in danger of being sucked back by the undertow of the next wave.

Oh the terrible sucking sound a wave makes as it rolls back. The breakers here are nothing like the breakers of Tahiti; but what if the bath turns over, or Laurence tries to sit up, or Christian doesn't notice in time, or she upsets it.

There's nothing to do but to lower myself into the water too. Christian is already way ahead. He has slowed down and is waiting until the last big wave of a group has formed, before he kicks himself forward with his flippers. I have never found it so difficult to cover six hundred feet before. Then, when I at last see him standing up, with the bath and flippers held above his head, the first big wave of the next series is on him: he just has time to run to the beach. What a drama.

Barbados. Fishing at night for flying fish. Nine in the evening: we are comfortably installed in our double bunk in the forecastle, reading by the warm glow of a kerosene lamp. The bay is calm, with only a light breeze, which prevents our opening the hatch completely in case the lamp blows out. Suddenly we become aware of things shooting across the water in every direction. Our two heads immediately pop out of the forehatch: five or six *gommiers*, the canoes without an outrigger but with fore-and-aft rigging, typical of the West Indies, are streaking across the bay in all directions.

They have only one sail, and obviously when you are poor anything will do to catch the wind: sacks, flour or salt bags, patchwork efforts, or plastic leaves. There are two men on each. The helmsman brandishes a torch of bamboo stuffed with rags soaked in kerosene, which he waves in the air. The fisherman in the bow, with amazing dexterity, catches the flying fish attracted by the light with a large net on the end of the pole. Not a word is spoken; there is silence except for the slight swish across the smooth surface of the water. Tomorrow at dawn the whole catch will be sold in under an hour. Because here, as elsewhere in the Antilles, there are plenty of fish in the lagoons but little in the markets. This is surprising: you never see a lagoon in an inhabited area without at least one underwater fisherman, with a canoe following him, and women who fish fully dressed, standing in the water up to their waists with their fishing lines—not to mention nets which they swim out to position. A Tahitian legend says that men are young porpoises who were placed on the shore by their dying mother: one can almost believe it. West Indians are descended from Africans, a mainland people, who as far as one can judge are not great water lovers. Although the sea is warm and there are not many sharks, they haven't got the sea in their blood.

"*Mamari.* Hullo, Ken. Good trip? How long did it take you?"
"Twenty-five days. No dead calms or storms. Marie is arriving by plane this week and we're getting married here."
A scene typical of any port where seafarers meet: we recount the details of our Atlantic voyages between snatches of song, with the help of Barbados punch and lemonade, guitars and harmonicas. The *Solmar* spent two days with her mast submerged, during the

65

storm we were in when we left the Canaries. The three tall, strong bearded men admit they felt very small on their beautifully varnished hull, which wouldn't right itself. All the contents had slipped to one side, and the water had begun to seep in. They pumped: the boat was heeled over at more than the maximum angle; it was impossible to steer, sleep, navigate, or even heat anything up. They thought they had had it. Tonight they are laughing noisily like people who are delighted and amazed to have escaped alive. They talk of selling the *Solmar.*

Ken gives us some sad news: the Swiss *Rhâ*—the couple with the little girl of two and a half—sank off Cape Verde. They hit a reef in the dark. Luckily they managed to get ashore in their dinghy. The boat was fully insured. They will go back to Switzerland to build another. Two years later I would meet them in the Antilles, chartering their new boat. What faith—we haven't got their confidence.

February already. And we wanted to be in Tahiti by the beginning of July to take advantage of the best sailing season before leaving for the Torres Strait. We're not racing; but we need to get to Tahiti soon to replenish the ship's funds. We're sure of being able to earn a bit there. It's sixteen months since we were last working and our budget has to be squeezed to cover the bare essentials.

Our supplies consist primarily of things it is essential to have if one is not to starve: large quantities of rice, corned beef, sardines, or pilchards for the days when there is no fresh fish; potatoes, sacks of onions, chickpeas or split peas, pasta, lentils and haricot beans. The only sweet thing we've got is white sugar, although we should have a lot of cookies, chocolate, canned puddings, canned and dried fruit, and candy, so that we could nibble at them day and night to prevent our feeling exhausted: one is always busy on a boat and always hungry.

On our last evening in Barbados we have our first Tahitian meal on board the *Alpha:* raw fish with coconut milk, yams, fried bananas, white and violet taro, breadfruit roasted on the Primus, sweet potatoes and fried fish, and as much coconut milk as we could want. It only takes a few seconds to get the fiber off the coconuts with a sharp point; then you cut the nut into perfect halves with two or three short, sharp blows, and squat and grate the coconut to extract the milk. In Tahiti the coconut grater is often fixed on a sort of stool, which makes a characteristic knocking sound. How often my sister and I had to stop fishing in the river when we were children, when this knocking started up all round us, telling that it was time for a meal: it is a sound as characteristic as the *angelus* in French villages.

Today we're so delighted at having coconut milk again that we rub it all over our bodies and in our hair, and Christian drinks half a glass of it.

"Take care—it's a laxative."

The only large fish we have found is a shark. We've never tasted shark meat and Christian is eager to try it as they eat it here. It's a bit tough for our liking, but our guests fall on it eagerly. The table setting is very simple: a *pareo* with two big plates, two soup plates, and four odd bowls for the eight of us. As we've only got three forks, we have to use our fingers. We drink orange-leaf tea and lemonade. It's good to be sitting around a table with friends after a month at sea.

6

A Sailor's Paradise

Laurence is lying in the cockpit, staring at the mainsheet. As the trade wind always blows in the same direction, we continue to sail westward. But we will come back to Barbados in two—or three? —years' time.

Today we start coasting from island to island, which is pleasant because we can come into a harbor every night, as on the Côte d'Azur. The West Indies are a sailor's paradise. Wind all year round, islands within sight of each other, white sands, green lagoons, coconut trees, sun, and hardly any tides. There are a few reefs, but they are generally around islands that rise steeply from the water. You just keep your eyes open and climb to the masthead from time to time. The dangerous times are at night, when you're tired, or when you're sailing into the sun and the sea shines so brightly that you can't distinguish the different-colored patches that indicate a shoal.

I love arriving at an island sheltered by a reef. A bar of coral is a marvelous breakwater, protecting the land from the fury of the sea and its inhabitants from large fish. Without reefs many Pacific islands would no longer exist.

We have to repair the sail, because while we were peacefully sleeping we jibed: the improvised boom, a broom handle to keep the jib sails boomed out, has cut right through the mainsail and torn it. We haven't a spare.

Didier is in the crosstrees to tell us the general direction in which to sail. From the foredeck I can take care of the details, signaling when to avoid small clumps of coral and estimating the depth of the water quickly. Union Island and Palm Island, a few miles apart, have the ring of white foam round them that indicates a protective coral reef. We nose up to the latter at a reasonable distance to find a way through.

"Hard-a-starboard."

"Hard-a-port."

What a slalom. The *Alpha* is like a toy. We play with her like a sailskiff, go about in a trice, skim over the sea, beat up to windward. Then the channel: fairly wide and with hardly any current. We tack up it in the broiling sun, without using the engine, to a wooden causeway where a friendly West Indian signals us to moor. A line fore and aft to the jetty—a rare luxury, which we don't often come across on our travels. The West Indian is the caretaker of the Union Island yacht club. It is surprising to find a yacht club on this small island, which seems very primitive and thinly populated. There are a few sailskiffs drawn up on the shore and of course several water-ski boats in a beautiful boathouse.

Christian and Didier, armed with three-cornered needles especially made for use on heavy cotton sails with thread like meat string, are doing more harm than good to our mainsail: every time the needle goes through it tears the cloth in every direction. But what else can we do? We've broken endless fine needles doing a few inches of seam.

Union Island rises gently to a wooded summit, which dominates the plain, where the grass is cropped like a lawn. Here and there are great brown patches of barren earth. There is little fresh food available—only tropical vegetables and fruit, at reasonable prices. Fish you must catch yourself, and you have to hunt your own meat. There are wild goats in the bush. Didier and Christian go to have a look with the caretaker. Instead of a goat they bring back a grayish iguana. The caretaker says it is a great delicacy, better than rabbit, and they give it to him as a present. Far from making it into a stew, I suspect he went off to stuff it and sell it to a tourist for $60 to $100.

Union Island, like all the Lesser Antilles, is a favorite haunt of luxury American charter yachts. During our forty-eight-hour stay, several gleaming boats have stopped for lunch or for the night. Like the Trojan horse, they disgorge an army of tourists. With shrimp-pink skin, checked caps, dark glasses, white cardboard nose protectors, floral West Indian shirts, flowered shorts that don't fit, bare feet, and of course their cameras, which will enable them to take a good look at the scenery for the first time, when they get home.

On the beach, trodden by thousands of other tourists every day for years, the women cry: "Oh, darling! Look at this shell! Oh, darling! Look at this stone!" And they keep a broken shell or piece of coral to remind them of their unspoiled desert island. In the evening, after a hearty meal washed down with plenty of drink, the dinghies are filled to bursting with this merry throng. They hurry ashore, the boat heels over precipitously, they scream and fall fully dressed into the water, and go and sing on the beach, fortified by gallons of strong punch. The natural life.

It's the natural life for us too. As there are no goats, we stuff ourselves with crayfish, squid, delicious redfish, washed down with coconut milk and accompanied by sweet potatoes and violet taro.

After two hours' sailing we reach Palm Island. A wonderful beach of white sand around a lagoon where some stilt birds are standing. Four mountains plonked down in a doll's-house landscape look over the emerald green lagoon and the dark blue sea. On the slopes of the hills are four beautiful villas carved in the stone, which melt into the mountains. It all belongs to an American, whose son Jim is tall, fair-haired, and bronzed. Christian and Didier spend hours diving with him.

I cross the lagoon with Laurence and make a tour of the island.

70

Sea fans spread their black lace on the white sand. Smoothly rounded bits of driftwood with shapes like animals, polished and bleached by the sea, look as though they are about to move: you could almost stroke them. The sand is so fine and white that it's a pleasure to see Laurence tumble in it. In the afternoon, after a stupendous catch, the three men go out goat hunting. They're optimistic, but I can't think where they would hide in this treeless landscape. I prudently prepare some fish—which is just as well because they come back without any goats and there are now five of them. They have invited a couple they met to share our second Tahitian meal. To complete our happiness, these two are flying to Paris tomorrow and will post our films to be developed and telephone Christian's family for us. A telephone call, hearing the voice of someone who has seen us and shared a meal with us, is one of the best presents we can give our family during the voyage.

Still the marvelous trade wind. Ideal sailing weather. We've no desire to stay in port.

Bequia is one of the prettiest of the Grenadine Islands. We are approaching it by moonlight, slowly, all ears and eyes. Tonight the full moon has kept me awake. It's good to think in the vast silence of the night. A silence filled with an intense but diffused humming, so that one doesn't know if it comes from within oneself or without. This uncertainty, the way one's organic and spiritual life mingles with the natural world around one, gives rise to ecstasy, and a great sense of anguish—pain at being infinitely small in the immense universe where we are both masters and of no more consequence than dust. At such moments, at sea, you feel as though you are losing all consciousness, existing beyond thought. But in a quiet harbor you hold your breath and enjoy the sensation to the fullest. When you are safe you can afford to feel scared.

"Hi, *Alpha!* Are you French?"

Admittedly you couldn't tell from our flag now: the red has unraveled, thread by thread.

Catherine is dark with lovely blue eyes. She is a professional pianist. She and Jean Flamanc charter their boat, working for eighteen months with an agency that sends them tourists. A forty-foot boat that can sleep two passengers, four if necessary, can be hired out, according to the standard of comfort it offers, for between $500 and $700 dollars a week, plus $6 a day per person for meals. It seems too good to be true, but Jean and Catherine are longing for a real holiday. We would understand what they felt like only too well after we had done this kind of work ourselves, on our new boat.

It's an endless infernal round. Five o'clock get up. While the tourists sleep, Catherine does the housework quietly, washes the deck and prepares a proper full-scale breakfast. This takes about two hours. Breakfast lasts till nine-thirty. Then the "guests" get dressed at their leisure and go on deck. Meanwhile Jean has completed the departure formalities, checked that they have enough water and fuel, weighed anchor and hoisted the sails. Catherine washes up, makes the beds, and tidies the cabins. At about ten-thirty or eleven o'clock, iced whiskey is served on deck and Catherine prepares lunch, a cold meal, which is served on deck at about twelve-thirty. More washing-up, and you drop anchor in a pretty bay. More maneuvering, formalities, etc. You then take the tourists ashore in the dinghy and lead them to the "souvenir" shop or leave them on the beach for a while. Catherine buys fresh food, bread. When she gets back to the yacht it's at least three o'clock. She has to prepare tea, which means a home-made cake or biscuits, for five o'clock. You take them all back to the dinghy, then transport them out to the yacht again. Catherine then must peel vegetables, prepare the meat, make another cake. Because in the evening there's the sacred dinner hour—or rather the damned dinner hour. There must always be an elaborate meat dish and a home-made dessert. This entails a lot of work, especially on a boat. The tourists have time to change, set their hair, and do their makeup, arrange the shells they've found on the beach. The meal goes on till 11 P.M. More washing-up and then you have to chat or play cards with them before you can go to bed.

That goes on for months and months without a break, with no private life except for a few hours together between midnight and 5 A.M. After that you need a holiday.

The bank comes today. The bank here is a little wooden boat that comes around twice a week. This morning it's moored along-

72

side a schooner unloading cement. We leave our anchor chained to a buoy, and go alongside to change a traveler's check. The bank boat can't be more than twelve meters long and looks rather old and rotten. When I think of the difficulty involved in attacking the English bank train! Jumping ashore, I go to get some bread from a nice fat old West Indian woman, who makes it the French way. A lovely surprise—it's hot and smells delicious.

The sun is setting. There are some old schooners lying aground on the beach with their beautiful long black hulls. Streaks of green cut across the pink-and-red sky. The colors change every minute, melting and fading into one another. At the instant when the sun disappears behind the horizon, when the sky is still bluey-green and the vegetation already black, a red flame seems to leap from the silken surface of the water for a few seconds, licking the motionless boats, changing them into dark shadow-lantern silhouettes against the green sky. Then the light suddenly vanishes, leaving the sky dark and studded with stars.

I always bring Laurence up to see the sunsets. At five months old she would point to the fiery horizon of her own accord, her eyes shining with delight.

It's so easy to learn how to be happy.

At St. Vincent, having completed the arrival formalities, we go fishing in a bay with very steep cliffs. On our return we moor at the quay, which is high and difficult to reach. The town is completely dead by 6 P.M., very ugly and dark. There are villas, which were clearly once pretty but which are now seedy, left to rot by their occupants. The people in the street look aggressive; there are no whites. It's the only West Indian island where we had the strange and unpleasant sensation of being a hated race that was not wanted there. It was a great relief to get back to our home, our *Alpha*— our little bit of France. All these British islands that have obtained their independence are extremely poor. The plantations taken over by the West Indians have been abandoned and there are hardly any schools. The young are bored and some of their ways of killing time are not very healthy. There are still lovely coconut and banana plantations. But no social organizations.

The island is very green, the valleys deep and wooded. It looks

73

as if wild goats would be there. We have to hug the coast for a bit as there's not a breath of wind. We find a deep bay running back inland, with two peaks towering above it—La Soufrière Bay. It does have a sulfurous atmosphere. We drop anchor 150 feet from the beach with a stern line around a coconut palm. Luckily there is a little river. While Laurence plays with mossy stones, I wash our sheets in the soft water.

All hands on deck at 7 A.M. The wind has got up early but is blowing from St. Lucia, where we are headed. The *Alpha* is sailing well into the wind and we make for our last Grenadian island. Coming into the bay of St. Lucia we meet the *Anjarro,* a charter boat. We've caught an enormous red mullet, the finest we've ever had—and are invited to join the barbecue on the beach, adding our catch to the lamb and chicken.

The next morning, although we got to bed very late, Laurence wakes us as usual. At nine, as the wind gets up, our sails are hoisted and the *Alpha* is off again.

As we go along the coast toward the port of Castries, we discover a channel that seems to disappear inland. You can see the inlet coming from St. Lucia, but it must be invisible coming from Castries or Martinique. Curious as always, we go about and sail up the channel, which leads to a marvelous deep, wide bay, at the foot of an almost uninhabited valley—Nelson Bay. It was here that the admiral hid his entire fleet, surprising the French as they sailed from Martinique.

No great sailing ships or warships today, but a comfortable motorboat with some friendly French people on board. We share our lunch. Jean-Pierre is returning to Paris this week: he will telephone Manouche, Christian's godmother, to give the family our news.

Perfect weather, sailing as if in a dream. With a good wind on the quarter and the sea almost flat, we skim along at six knots toward Fort-de-France in Martinique.

The sea and happiness.

You have to really take in this weather—feel it, absorb it, in silence, and let it be engraved on your memory so that you'll remember it for a long time. The sails are full, the wind doesn't

74

waver, Gigi purrs contentedly on her pins, the sun is just the right heat.

At Fort-de-France we find the *Erna,* the *Inconnu,* which we left behind at Cannes, the steel *Pingouin,* which we haven't seen since Casablanca—and our mail. Civilization.

Two-thirds of the thirty or so letters waiting for us date from the time of Laurence's birth, and Christmas. The questions about the preparations for our voyage are meaningless now, and I think the only appropriate reply we could make would be to quote from the telegram from our Uncle Pierre: "Bravo. First lap safely over."

This has been the easiest part from the point of view of navigating, but perhaps the hardest for Laurence and me. The problems everyone experiences in a relationship, the gulf between me-Laurence and Christian-the-boat, mean that I often feel neglected and alone. I have many times, I must admit, like everyone else, I imagine, asked myself if I haven't made a mistake, if I wouldn't do better to go ashore, earn my living somewhere, with my child, rather than leading this life in which Christian and I have so little time for each other. I find it hard to remember these doubts now, my desire to escape. I remember one day, when I was particularly tired and discouraged, I was only deterred by the thought that, if I went ashore and found work, I would have to put Laurence in a nursery school, and wouldn't see her all day.

The harmonious and united family we are today did not happen easily or as a matter of course. I see our life as the slow and difficult formation of a couple, of a family unit that the boat and the sea have helped us create.

Fort-de-France. Didier and I are looking for work: our funds are at rock bottom. But it's rather difficult to get a job when we don't know when we'll be leaving—possibly in a week, or a month, or six months. When the wind is right the *Alpha* will sail on toward the sun again.

After about three weeks Didier is taken on as a sales representative for a wine company, and Christian and I give sailing lessons. One fine morning, with Jacqueline, Marie-Odile, Jean-Claude, and Jean Pierre on board, we set off to spend the weekend at Pigeon Island, a little island to the north of St. Lucia. Our friend Ricky had told us how to approach the island—we have no chart. It's easy in daylight, but you mustn't make a mistake and approach it from the north, where there is an easily identifiable rock, instead of the south. In our hurry to be off our little plan gets lost.

The day goes well. No one is sick, it's lovely weather, and we get to Castries at about five o'clock. There's nothing attractive about Castries. We are unanimous in deciding not to spend the night there. Pigeon Island is quite near and we reset the sails. Ricky talked of white sands, palm trees, and marvelous places for underwater fishing. The *Alpha* is nosing toward Pigeon Island, when the tropical night—there is no twilight in the Tropics—falls suddenly and completely. There's no moon until midnight or 1 A.M. Pigeon Island is a black line against the black sea and sky, directly ahead of us. How far? We have no idea.

At about nine o'clock, getting more and more anxious, I start boldly humming jolly sea chanteys and, very discreetly, anchor Laurence and her cot securely. You never know—a sudden bump; Laurence is only five months old.

The wind has dropped slightly and to save time Christian has the engine going. A one-cylinder diesel in a steel hull makes quite a noise. We sing at the tops of our voices on deck, in the dark. Jean-Claude peers into the darkness from the foredeck—one can't see anything at all. And it's the first time he's been at sea.

The din of the engine, and the crescendo of our voices . . .

"France, do you remember from which side one should approach the island?"

"I think there was a dangerous rock on the north."

"What are those lights over there? Boat masts?"

"Oh, we'd better not make for the lights; there probably isn't a harbor there. They'd confuse us."

And we swing round to the north. Where the rock is. It's incredible how stupid one can be.

Crash—a thunderous noise, of metal crashing against a reef as hard as granite. The waves throw us violently to starboard, right across the rocky ledge.

I have to cry, "Christian, Christian!" thinking "Laurence . . ."

But I am at the tiller, with the engine full a-stern, the tiller hard a-port.

The waves have subsided a little, but we have to hurry because they won't be like that for long. Christian jumps into the water, and heaves with all his might while I rev the engine. My heart's in my mouth. Laurence is still asleep and not crying. That's the most important thing. The *Alpha* moves off the shoal of rock, and I can breathe again. A fairly small breaker knocks us back a bit. Christian shoves as hard as he can, and climbs aboard, dashes past me to the tiller. There is the roar of a huge wave as it forms—the *Alpha* cuts through it neatly at right angles, and we are saved. We must have hit the rock at least six times, hard.

I slam open the roof and go down to the saloon to light the storm lantern. Shout: "The water's coming in. It's up to my ankles."

Laurence is still peacefully asleep down there. We take up the floor and begin handing a chain of buckets, which are quicker than our bilge pump. It's exhausting work, especially when the water never goes down. We can't stop for a second. We pass the buckets from hand to hand, inches from Laurence's cot and still she doesn't wake up. It's a great blessing, because I don't think I could bear to hear her cry just now. The fact that she's asleep gives me strength and I feel reassured, as if nothing terrible could happen while she's sleeping.

Anyway there's no time to think. Bent over the bilge I fill two buckets one after the other without a break—a red two-gallon one and a smaller blue one. The person behind me takes the red bucket and passes it to the "emptier" in the cockpit. Jean-Claude, in front of me, takes the blue bucket and empties it through the fore-hatch. We change places every quarter of an hour, because it makes you feel giddy. Christian is at the tiller and doing all he can to force on the *Alpha* toward Castries. The water has stopped rising in the cabin, but is not getting any lower. We reach Castries at about midnight. The water's stopped coming in and the bottom is dry. The mud has stopped up the hole, which seems to be in the keel. But where? And how big is it? We'll have to wait till tomorrow to see.

In the meantime, after cleaning up down below, we hold a

meeting. There are several possibilities for getting back, if the *Alpha* has to be laid up in Castries—which might be difficult anyway. Then the skipper says that in the circumstances no one will be expected to pay his share of the expenses. But he is immediately interrupted by protestations: "We wouldn't hear of it."

"It was a risk we all took."

"It was a great experience and we don't regret it at all."

"You must let us pay our share. It's your job."

I'll never forget those words.

Then we go to bed. Laurence, who has been constantly shoved around amidst all the uproar, is still sleeping soundly.

Christian and I have nightmares all night, about huge holes in the hull, water filling the cabin, Laurence still asleep in the water while the boat goes down in the dark, with water everywhere, all round us. Yet it's the first time the *Alpha* has been so still, with her keel firmly planted in the mud.

The next day, as always, the weather is magnificent. As soon as it's light Christian dives down to see what the damage is. Some dents on the starboard side, below the waterline. A tiny crack about half an inch wide in the root of the keel. That's all. The cement around the ballast came away from the steel, letting the water in.

Ideally the part of the keel containing the ballast should be isolated from the rest of the boat by welded steel plates: the water wouldn't have come in then. The crack is two plates up. It's always there that we hit anything first. We must reinforce it.

For the time being Christian dives down and applies a bit of hot pitch to the crack; it sets hard and fills the crack beautifully. We've gotten off lightly, but what is more annoying is that the rudder post is out of line and it's difficult to work the tiller. We'll have to go into dry dock to set it right—and that'll be expensive. Just for good measure the accelerator lever is broken. Christian sets up a pulley and a length of nylon rope, a system which we use for a year, after several unsuccessful attempts to solder on a lever.

Now that there is no risk of sinking, we set off for Pigeon Island again in blazing sunshine. Seeing the place in daylight, we are amazed to have escaped so lightly. A wooden boat would have been splintered to pieces between the ferocious waves and the iron-hard rock. Our steel hull saved us, and yet we only had three millimeters of freeboard above the waterline. Anyway, one must obviously approach the bay from the south, where we saw the yachts yesterday. Ricky had warned us—it was just one of those stupid accidents.

Back in Fort-de-France, we decide we must dry dock the *Alpha* —but how are we to pay for it? Maybe we could beach her, like the Grenadine schooners? It's an idea—but there's hardly any tide in Martinique. We need a sheltered beach where we can get her welded—and we'll need electricity. We'll also have to empty the boat of most of her contents, and live elsewhere for a few days. And then there'll be problems with the mast and rigging. It's far from an ideal solution.

We go to tell Germaine and Ricky our troubles and ask their advice. We have a fruit-juice cocktail before dinner, submerged to our necks in a heated swimming pool at their lovely villa. The pool is the only daily relaxation Ricky allows himself. He's an extraordinary man: when he was still in school he spent the long vacation underwater, cutting metal posts with a blow torch. It's extremely hard work, for which you must have an excellent constitution. It was in this way that he got his first boat—a *gommier.* Since then he has started numerous businesses, one of them being *Jalousies Martiniquaises,* which he manages, while bringing up his large and charming family. Germaine and Ricky are an exceptional couple, and our dinner with them was immensely soothing.

Naturally, Ricky has welding equipment. Of course he has men to work it. And he also has a friend, Mr. Grant, who has a yard where the boat can be hauled up. He telephones him at once to ask if we could pay a reduced rate. We understand that it will be about 150 francs if we don't take too long. One hundred fifty francs is incredibly cheap, but it will make a terrible hole in our budget all the same. We say we'll think about it.

At dawn, the *Alpha* is hauled up the slipway and into dry dock. We've got twenty-four hours to repair and careen her. Ricky is going to send us his welding gear for the keel, and his men will also take care of the rudder. Armed with scrapers, Christian and I scrub and scrub—we remove seaweed, moss, and barnacles which have stuck to the boat in spite of the anti-fouling we put on in Casablanca.

Laurence sleeps or plays in the cabin, unperturbed by the noise and heat of the careening.

After the scrapers, we use wire wool, then sandpaper, and finally scouring powder and a scrubbing brush. It doesn't sound very difficult, but with only the two of us going at high speed, in the tropical heat, it's grueling work. You have to keep bending over and reaching up to rub and scrape. When the hull is clean, we put on two good coats of quick-drying minium.

By eleven the three men are there with the welding gear. While they are strongly reinforcing the root of the keel, Christian pours some pitch between the cement and the hull to prevent any risk of corrosion, and puts a new layer of cement in the bilge.

At midday the crew of a large fishing boat, which is also hauled up there, bring us some hot food—a kindness that I can only repay with smiles, because they speak in a South American Spanish. And Mr. Grant brings us a magnificent lettuce from his garden, with the air of one apologizing for bringing so little. But in the torrid heat of the dry dock, nothing could have been more welcome than the sight of the crisp green leaves.

At about four o'clock Christian takes out the rudder and tries to straighten the post with the help of the men. We'll put it back later. Meanwhile I finish putting on a coat of white paint with a roller.

Mr. Grant can hardly believe we were on the Pigeon Island's rocks: "In twenty years, I've never known a boat get off them. One can see from the dents that you hit the rocks hard, but there is hardly any damage; it's incredible. And not a spot of rust or electrolysis on the hull, although in parts the paint obviously wore off long ago."

"That's thanks to Bernard Moitessier. He advised us to place anodes all round the keel, fore and aft, as rust is caused by electrolysis."

At nine, after another meal from our neighbors on the fishing boat, we put on the second coat of white paint and paint in the waterline. What a day.

Next day at 5 A.M., we put on the anti-fouling. When Mr. Grant opens the yard at 7 we're ready to go. The *Alpha* is hoisted in the cradle, all newly painted and gleaming. The slipway is free for us to pass. And, when Christian asks what we owe him for the slip, Mr. Grant says simply that there's nothing to pay.

We will never forget his kind expression, how sweet he was with Laurence, and his generosity toward us.

Nothing is worse on a yacht than having to sail on a date set in advance. When you've chosen to live on a boat, you are irrevocably committed to the caprices of the wind, the sea, and the seasons. They give the orders, and decide when you can leave. You have the opposite attitude to the man who has subjugated nature, who crushes a mushroom under the wheels of his Jaguar, defies time and space in his plane, or counteracts a headache with a pill. At sea man becomes insignificant. You have no control over a wave or the wind. You make yourself small, erase yourself, wait till the storm is over, trying to control your boat as best you can, and yourself as best you can, doing your utmost to stay alive.

You don't challenge the sea or defy her. You listen, try to feel her mood if you can, and guess what she will do. You can love her, passionately, but she can make you afraid and harm you; she can be cruel. Even when you think you know her, you can never tell what she has in store for you.

But go we must, because Jacqueline's holiday begins today and she has decided to go sailing with us for a fortnight, and to go as far as she can with us. We embark at eight in the morning in the quiet little harbor behind the fort. There are some white caps outside—we're in for some fun and games.

Germaine has given us a complete medicine chest. En route for Dominica!

On rounding the point, we find there is a fresh breeze. There are flurries of wind all around us, but the strong gusts are from the east. It's odd seeing the wind making circles around us, ruffling the surface of the water in a strange way.

As soon as we are in the channel between Martinique and Dominica, the wind increases and we have to lower the jib quickly, hoist the storm jib, and reef the mainsail. The *Alpha* heels right over. Finally, we lower the mainsail, and reef the storm jib. Seasickness attacks all hands—only Laurence is spared—and I take some Marzine just in case. The troughs are three to four yards deep, but the waves are going in practically every direction, and we are shipping a green sea. In spite of his oilskin and three sweaters Christian is drenched to the skin. Didier too.

There are gusts and squalls with bright intervals all day. We're thankful to drop our trusty CQR anchor in La Soufrière Bay in Dominica. The water is very deep right up to the shore, which we reach by swimming. We munch some sprouting coconuts, which can be easily opened as soon as a shoot is growing from the husk. Inside there is a spongy, sweet, juicy substance—the seed—which is called the *uto* in Tahiti. My father calls it sugared cotton. Children love it, and so do we.

We are rocked mercilessly by a heavy swell all night. When we have a charter passenger on board, I always feel guilty if we can't offer them fine weather, particularly during the first few hours, because there must be nothing nastier than starting one's holiday by being violently seasick. I feel as embarrassed as if it were entirely my fault if there is bad weather the day our guests choose to come aboard. How can one explain that it's best to wait for favorable weather, that one must never feel hurried or pressed for time—that one must be like Saint-Exupéry's Little Prince, who said: "If I had fifty-three minutes to spare, I would walk quietly towards a fountain"?

In the morning Jacqueline insists she's had a very good night, and seems delighted. I feel reassured.

The rigging was severely strained in yesterday's wind, and the sails have come unsewn in several places. We have to spend over an hour mending them. While I wield my needle—which is tough work in this material—I remember Bernard Moitessier's sound advice to us to reinforce the fabric where the seams meet and at danger points. How stupid of us to be so careless. One always hopes that these things will happen to other people, not oneself. So, instead of swimming in the clear water here, we have to sew on patches. It's the chore I like least of all on board.

Here we are in the wide bay at Portsmouth. It's very deep, with a beach of dark gray volcanic sand. Ragged little children swim out to sell us a few oranges and bananas, and shriveled tomatoes the size of a gull's egg. Touched, we buy everything except the tomatoes. The kids seem to be only five, seven, and eight years old. They carry their wares in transparent nylon bags.

I suddenly see that the smallest is in tears on the beach. The two older ones look at us silently and despairingly. The bag with the tomatoes is being carried out to sea by the current, and has just gotten as far as the *Alpha*. I immediately jump into the sea, but quickly realize what the matter is: a horde of small jellyfish bite me all over. Poor little children. I manage to recover the tomatoes and the bag, and set out with Jacqueline and the children to a nearby village.

By the side of the trodden-earth path, pathetic hovels made of old packing cases, boxes, and rusty corrugated iron, propped against each other in miserable rows, provide scanty shelter for ragged children with distended bellies. The adults sit by the path and gossip. It's a fishing village, but they only fish from their boats, with a line or net, or more often, as everywhere in the West Indies, with traps: the fish swim into a lattice-work cage and can't get out.

Dominica has a very fertile volcanic soil where things grow well. There are plenty of trees and coconut palms. I can't understand why the people are so listless. It seems one could live well there on hardly anything, if one wanted to, with very little effort. So why don't they bother? Here too I got the impression that the Africans brought here long ago had never been able to adapt to their surroundings.

This morning Laurence has her first tooth. It's amazing, because I hadn't noticed it coming. She hasn't been dribbling or crying or seemed upset recently. Then this morning I saw this little hard white thing on the pink of her gum. Rushing to my child-care books, I see she is of legal age for a first tooth, that all is well and she has been spared a lot of trouble. This little tooth makes her seem very grownup all of a sudden. How quickly babies grow old. And yet I'm longing for her to be bigger.

A fairly strong wind takes us from Dominica to Îles des Saintes in three hours, and we get there just after sunset. The village of Terre de Haut is like a dream: Breton fishing boats of every color are drawn up on the sand all along the beach. Everything is in soft pastel colors, clearly delineated, clean and charming, gay or sober, simple but heartwarming. One has an irresistible desire to see it close to.

We go ashore to get bread. Little concrete paths wind between old French houses, each surrounded by a very low wall and a well-kept garden. There is nothing rich or ostentatious about them. Everything has the air of having been lovingly made, with a passionate desire to keep up the traditions and life style of ancestors who came here two hundred years ago. The Bretons never mixed with the West Indians from Terre de Bas. They intermarried and kept their blond hair and blue eyes, and they have also become rather inbred. Which is why the French warships that call here on their way to Tahiti are a welcomed distraction.

At six in the evening Terre de Haut is as lively as a fishing village in the South of France. Every night the sailors crowd into the only café in the port to drink or sing around large red- or green-covered tables, or hold animated discussions. The children are simply dressed, but very clean and well cared for. The young people have retained a certain distinction. They are not cowlike or soft, or alternatively brash. The determination to remain French in the West Indies is in their blood. They have the fierce patriotism of people who are cut off from their homeland.

When we've finished shopping we come round to anchor on the other side of the island, at Pain de Sucre. It's much more sheltered here than at the village. We moor alongside a wooden landing stage standing in six feet of water. The landing stage leads to a very white sandy beach below a lovely coconut plantation. Under the palms is a large colonial-style house with wide verandas and outbuildings dotted here and there among the trees. It is very elegant and one can imagine a lady in a crinoline dress lying languidly on a chaise longue with a little black servant waving a large fan.

We'd like to spend a fortnight in this sheltered bay. The water is green, and when there's a wind, everything looks wild and tormented, with crude colors that contrast strangely with those of the evening before. We feast on fish, crabs, and lobsters.

But if we want to get to Tahiti this year we must press on. As we are heaving up the anchor a Zodiac comes alongside with officers on board from the *Rhin,* a French warship, which is on its way to Polynesia for the second series of atomic tests, the Force Alpha No. 2. It's an emotional moment for us meeting the *Rhin* in the Île des Saintes: when we were snapping instant photos in Tahiti to get our boat, there wasn't a sailor who didn't have one of our color photographs, of himself with a Tahitian girl and garlands of flowers, in his wallet. So seeing the *Rhin* again is like coming full circle: we're back where we started, having realized our dream. And the Force Alpha gives us a present—a tin of ship's biscuits. The sailors call them "war bread," and look surprised when I refer to them as "little cakes." As we're dining aboard the *Rhin,* we decide not to leave until tomorrow.

We sail from island to island on our way to Antigua, one of them a desert island, where we feel like Robinson Crusoe, and where Laurence can play for hours in the water. At Antigua there's an airport and Jacqueline will be able to fly back to Fort-de-France. We say *au revoir,* and sail on.

And at six o'clock on Thursday, April 25, we reach St. Barthélemy. It's a French port. The population is Breton and native West Indian. Unfortunately it's a gray day and we have only dispiriting, depressed memories of our last island in the Antilles. Yet the people there are extremely pleasant. It's upsetting; one wants to get them all away from there, away from their monotonous and limited existence, which isn't actively harmful but which doesn't make them very happy either.

At last we're on our way to Panama, to the Pacific. We begin to feel we're making a long voyage. The adventure is just beginning.

7

Patience in the Doldrums

Our only chart of the Caribbean is a pilot's chart—showing winds and currents—given to us by a cargo boat. We won't sight land again until we get to Panama. At least that's what we hope. Ricky has strongly advised us not to get shipwrecked on an island belonging to Venezuela, because we could end up in prison. It happened to one of his friends not long ago.

On our way to Tahiti at last. I've had time to forget what it's like out on the open sea. It's incredible how many boats that have set out to go around the world finish up in the West Indies. Hundreds have stopped there for good, attracted by the easy life. Not to mention those who have been disheartened by their first long passage—across the Atlantic—and who have put their boats up for sale and begun to dream about mountain châlets.

Now the serious part is beginning.

We are in the Caribbean and hope it will be less daunting than the people who gave it their name. Judging by the pilot chart there'll never be a lack of wind. There should be a strong prevailing wind of force four or five along the whole route, with about nil percent of calms. The currents are mostly favorable to us. But the area is very crowded—a funnel in which steamers, yachts, and merchantmen congregate from all sides, going toward the canal. You have to keep your eyes open. We know from experience that a light is not enough.

Christian tries in vain all day to get Washington on our old radio receiver. He can't get a time signal from anywhere. We must know what the Greenwich Mean Time is, because the only chronometer we have is a watertight watch.

We get back into the rhythm of a long voyage, nibbling ship's biscuits and wishing we had a whole cargo of them. They relieve seasickness, anxiety, and that hollow feeling in your stomach.

We can get Cuba clearly on our receiver, and are lectured all day about the horrible Yankees, but can't get a time check. We must try something else—it's getting urgent. The skipper reckons we are about ninety miles from the last little Dutch island. We have two compasses. One is inside, at the head of the captain's bunk, the other on deck. The latter doesn't work and swivels crazily in all directions. We can't think why.

Laurence feeds hungrily. I have to rest more, and fight desperately against my growing lassitude. Laurence has a perfect grasp of the ideal way to spend the first few days at sea: eat and drink well, keep warm, and sleep as much as you can. She's never sick. She has a sea-water bath every day in the cockpit.

Catastrophe! I had put her bedding out on deck, with the empty crib on the cockpit bench. When I go to get it, it has disappeared. I'm terribly upset. Luckily there's still the mattress. I sew some strong material onto it and a bit of fishnet, which I hook on screws. It's less attractive and comfortable, and not even transportable. And we can't buy anything else until we get to Tahiti. I, who had always dreamed of a pretty baby's bedroom. I've stuck some simple drawings on the varnished ceiling, which is only fifteen inches above her head, to brighten it up a bit. Her only toys are a plastic counting frame, three rings on a chain, and three little rubber animals.

Nothing on the wireless. A broken connection, probably. The days pass. The sea is growing stormier. It's miserable in this weather not to be sure of our bearings, which Christian can only judge from the time we had before. We could be twenty or thirty miles from our estimated position, that is, nearer to the coastline with its islands and dangerous shallows. Our badly patched sails are straining in the wind. Will they hold out as far as Tahiti?

Opening the hatch is impossible. Every time we open it a crack to crawl out, the skipper's bed is drowned in a flood of water. Still, we have no regrets.

Gigi is straining in the stormy sea. As well as being steep, the waves often hit us broadside. The *Alpha* has a violent movement, and our muscles strain all the time. We can't sleep properly.

So that Laurence can play in safety, I have fastened some sailcloth right across my bunk, and she holds happily onto it. She jumps on her fat little legs, but never loses her balance. Even when she moves around in the cabin, she never falls, in spite of the rolling motion of the boat, which makes us all hold on tightly. The waves are sweeping over the deck all the time, so she'll stay down below while this lasts.

Now the mainsail begins to tear. We lower it immediately and as sewing is impossible today, we hoist the red boomed-out storm jib. Christian takes the radio receiver to bits and finds a wire has come loose. Didier gets out the gas soldering iron, but loses the cap while putting in the refill. Overboard. So there's no hope of mending the receiver. A good example of how important an object can be at sea. The loss of this piece could cost us our lives.

All we know is that we don't know—within twenty miles—where we are. This is no fun! The sea is growing more stormy all the time and it's very difficult to keep on course. The waves crash against the bows. Didier has moved his bedding onto the floor in the saloon.

Should I have forced Laurence to lead this life? The permanent din, the violent jolts that the human body was not made to withstand. But is it worse than the Métro rumbling under Paris all night, the cars and polluted air, and frenetic people rushing about in towns?

In the week since we left St. Barthélemy, we've lost two good towing lines, a black oilskin, Gigi's wrench, Laurence's crib, two booms, and a torn jib. The engine has stalled, Gigi has just broken, and we can't mend the radio. It would be difficult to have a worse run of luck in so short a time.

We're taking turns at the helm—it's absolutely exhausting.

As we never sleep deeply, my nerves are in shreds. And no one can understand that who hasn't experienced it. You have to have felt like that to believe it. Why don't I regret having come? Why does the temptation to go ashore and live elsewhere remain only a vague impulse? Because adventure runs in my blood. Because I'm too tired to think. It was only later I understood that basically it was because I couldn't imagine life any other way: you can't put a price on a sunset in the northern Galápagos Islands; it is worth a lot of sacrifices.

The bread's finished today: the rest is all green and must be thrown away. The bananas are finished. And so is the large foresail: I took the tiller while Christian took our bearings. Two waves in quick succession came up behind me from astern. I didn't react quickly enough, we jibed and the jib split in two right down the center seam, which came completely loose. Luckily the mainsail has been mended meanwhile: we hoist it at once. But it seems very fragile in this weather. Where are we? The thought obsesses us.

This morning we got to within thirty yards of a German cargo boat that must have been on its way from Panama, to ask them where we are. Some men on the deck stared at us through their binoculars. Christian made signals, which they didn't understand. Finally I went on deck with Laurence and semaphored SOS. They went calmly on their way. If we had been more urgently in need of help I don't think they would have acted any differently.

It's even more depressing because the sky is overcast, the wind is increasing in strength, and the sea is rising, rising. The water is dirty, muddy, and full of all kinds of debris: bits of packing cases, plastic bottles, tree trunks on which seabirds perch with shrill cries.

We have only our ten square yards of canvas, two storm jibs

goosewinged out, one on the forestay, the other in place of the mainsail, held by a firmly secured broomstick. But with the wind mostly force eight or nine this frail boom will probably break and tear the sail any minute now. So the skipper takes off our only boom, the proper one, but makes a false move and the spar falls into the water. And we're running before the wind.

"CHRISTIAN!"

He's in the water. I scream at the top of my lungs. My voice gets lost, piping in the wind, which is howling like a pack of wolves. A fearful agony constricts my throat, my stomach. Every tenth of a second counts, and yet I do nothing. I do nothing because any movement would be time lost, lost forever, because I can still see Christian. As if my seeing him could prevent his disappearing, keep him within our grasp.

Didier and I have thrown him the mooring line, which is always coiled in the stern. By some awful mishap it wasn't secured. I thought Didier was taking care of it and he was probably counting on me to do the only possible thing—take a turn around the mooring cleat.

Our two storm jibs are boomed out forward. There is a strong wind and the troughs of the waves are six or seven yards deep. The *Alpha* is riding out the gale well. It is impossible to heave to at once without sheeting in the sails. And it is out of the question to luff up and go about in this weather: even if we were hove to, the current is so strong that we'd be no better off. We can see tree trunks sailing past us.

Each tenth, hundredth of a second is vital now. I am panicking; my thoughts and reflexes are frozen. Everything rushes through my head wildly: rope on the box bunk—it would take time to go down for it, I'd lose Christian from sight; throw anything that will float —the buoy in front of me—but my body won't respond. Why? Didier isn't doing anything either; he must be numbed too, or panicking, it comes to the same thing.

Christian has caught hold of the log. The log line, a nylon line a few millimeters in diameter, secured to the boat by a small bit of metal, is not exactly designed for hauling a man on board. Why doesn't one of us throw a line to him now? Because we both think that the log line will give? That it will be too late anyway? Why?

90

Am I even capable of thought? Am I aware of the fact that Christian's life hangs on a log line?

I didn't even think "man overboard," which as far as I am concerned is synonymous with certain death. It's a black hole, nothingness. I am outside of time. I've even forgotten Laurence.

Christian is an exceptional swimmer. He is gaining inch by inch. His muscles will break. Luckily he only has bathing trunks on, and has strong lungs. He raises his head from the water as little as possible so as to offer the least resistance in the raging, glaucous, dirty sea.

The sky is black, the wind whistles in the rigging, and the *Alpha* is straining. Each second seems like an hour. I can't breathe, I'm not trembling: I am beyond all reaction. I stand unmoving, my eyes on Christian. My mind and body are frozen.

Christian climbs aboard. Everything goes hazy. "Why didn't you take a turn round the cleat?" He doesn't even seem angry. Did he realize the position he was in?

Why did he jump overboard to rescue the boom in such a heavy sea? He wanted to get a line round the boom in the water and haul it up. There's always a line coiled in the stern: why wasn't it made fast? It all happened so quickly it seems incredible. Why didn't we take a turn around the cleat? It was an unpardonable, inconceivable error.

Christian is safely on board.
Christian is safely on board.
Christian is safely on board.

The strongest impulse at times like this is to shout "Help!" but no one could have heard and one realizes how helpless one is in the middle of the ocean.

Was our fatigue responsible? We knew very well what we ought to have done; it was quite easy, and yet we didn't do it. We foresaw everything except the panic that hit us like a sledgehammer paralyzing the nervous system.

The broomstick of course breaks as expected, and we hoist and reef the mainsail. But one of the main seams gives: how will we reach Panama? Everything is sopping on board. Our sweaters are dripping wet in spite of our oilskins. Didier is very tired and beginning to feel seasick. Christian replaces him at the tiller to give him a chance to rest. We still don't know where we are. The weather is appalling. Squall follows squall, and it's impossible to get a true navigational fix because the sky is perpetually overcast. We are merely surviving on board—trying to think as little as possible and not to talk, because at such times one can only talk about one's worries.

But we are cheered by Laurence with her smiles, her chattering, the progress she makes each day, her radiant health, her childish voice, and two little white teeth, gleaming like pearls.

When we wake up it's dead calm, which seems incredible. It's like being in port. We go up on deck in the sun. Christian starts the engine and repairs Gigi. The log indicates that we are doing four knots under power: the hull is covered with weed in spite of the speed we've been making and the anti-fouling gear. Next day the wind gets up a little. We pass two merchantmen, which signal to us that we're on the right course; this reassures us a bit.

We're brusquely awakened at 2 A.M. Christian has started the engine. Before us, only one or two miles off, in the brilliant moonlight lies the rocky coast of South America—black and aggressive, like a sinister tomb. So we must be twenty miles from the position we calculated on the incorrect time. If Christian had been asleep we would have landed up at the edge of the dense forest—which smells, surprisingly strongly, of chlorophyll—far from civilization and help. But somehow our skipper always instinctively senses danger.

Unable to sleep, we hug the coast until dawn. As it grows light we see several boats are on the same course as ourselves, and we reach Panama safely.

The Canal Zone is a bit of America dumped down in the heavy, humid equatorial heat. It rains there every day. We make ourselves at home for the evening in the Cristóbal yacht club, a wooden building with a large veranda-restaurant that extends onto the landing stages. We have a lovely hot shower to get the salt off our skin. The next day the two men go off: by law one must have five adults on board to go through the canal, plus a special pilot.

Christian and Didier are helping a neighboring yacht, the *Fugue,* who will help us tomorrow.

I seize the opportunity to clean the boat. The oil lamps and Primus smoked a lot crossing the Caribbean, and the ceiling is gray. Meanwhile Laurence explores the deck on all fours. I'm not afraid she'll fall overboard because she never goes anywhere without testing each handhold carefully. She's incredibly careful, and she's still only seven months old.

But I have to retrieve her from the *Skaffie,* a twenty-one-foot yacht of 4.8 tons, belonging to Dee Dee and Jim, who have decided to sail to the West Indies with two little kittens—the kittens that attracted Laurence. The *Skaffie* will have fun if they meet the same weather we've just had. I don't think we'd have the courage to go back just now. It's a bit reckless of them to sail in that direction at this time of year, when there is a 99 percent chance of a strong head wind.

At seven o'clock, as the men are not yet back, Dee Dee and Jim invite me to the yacht club for a French steak: steak with potatoes and a green salad. Delicious. Laurence, sitting in a high chair for the first time in her life, watches us and covers herself with a delicious potato puree topped with grated cheese and fresh butter.

At about eleven, the men have all arrived back by train, and want to go to bed at once because it will be our turn early in the morning. I learn that the *Fugue,* which left at 7 A.M., arrived at Balboa at 6 P.M. In the last lock the current wedged them against a huge barge and they couldn't get free. It was funny in retrospect. It took them an hour and a half to get back by train, and cost a dollar each. It costs eleven dollars for the boat to go through, which is very reasonable, because one might be the only boat in a lock, and we make as much work for the canal as a steamer.

Wednesday, May 15. The pilot comes on board. It is obligatory that we be stationed as follows: Didier and one American each with a line in the bow, Christian and the second American each with a line in the stern, with myself at the tiller. The pilot directs operations and takes over the tiller if any difficulties arise. So Laurence

93

will have to spend the day below, in the cabin, in spite of the torrid heat. It's impossible to keep her on deck; she can only come up to be fed.

After our six hundred locks in Europe, we're not too worried about going through the canal. And Christian and I have also been through it several times on steamers. It's familiar territory for us. Which doesn't detract from the violence of the currents or the backwash.

We feel terribly small in the vast lock, with hawsers that seem to go on forever; the safety of the *Alpha* depends on the strength of these strands.

Christian is on edge when he has to hand over the tiller, in this strong current, to a pilot used to large cargo boats, who admits it's the first time he's taken a yacht through. Right in the middle of Lake Gatun we run out of fuel. We continue under canvas, while the pilot on his walkie-talkie set asks for a refill. Less than two hours later, a motorboat brings us five gallons of fuel. We haven't lost very much time. Lake Gatun is very turbulent, and we'd hate to fall in the water for fear of hungry caymans.

We get through the locks without a hitch, and moor at the Balboa yacht club at about six. We can stay there free for ten days. A motorboat with a pilot—also free—is at our disposal to take us ashore from seven in the morning until seven at night. But tonight we've no desire to go ashore—we only want to sleep.

We've got a very crowded program for our stay in Panama—ten days—because the visa given to us for going through the canal expires after that date. We need to obtain a visa for the Galápagos Islands; buy a radio receiver that works; change the jib halyard; learn about lights in the Galápagos from a neighboring boat; fill up with water and fuel; and stock up with provisions for at least four months, because we can't be sure of finding what we want in the Galápagos. We also ought to take advantage of the tide to careen the hull, find a good boom and fishing lines. Quite a full program.

As far as the visa is concerned, we certainly ought to have gotten it elsewhere. As both Ecuador and Panama change governments fairly frequently, the Ecuadorian consul never gets paid—so he pays himself. It's quite a comedy. Normally a visa of this sort costs only about $3. The consul is squat, plump, and thick-lipped,

94

and the price of a visa in fact depends on his mood, his degree of lucidity at the time, and the yachtsman's appearance. Christian must look far too wealthy because he starts by asking for $35. You have to bargain. But the little man won't listen to us. I explain in Spanish that I've got a baby, that I might have to see a doctor in the Galápagos Islands, and that anyway we can't pay $35. He shakes his head, stubborn and churlish as a mule: "There's no doctor in the Galápagos."

Which is incorrect because there's one at the American base. In an emergency a plane can fly you to America straightaway. The little man continues: "All right, thirty dollars."

We leave, deciding to abandon the Galápagos and go directly from Panama to the Marquesas Islands. We write to all the family telling them this. But on the evening before we are to leave the consul suddenly says it will be $17. We ask for a receipt, but he goes scarlet with rage. So we decide to leave it, although it's half what he first asked.

Panama turns out to be a very friendly port for us. An extremely distinguished gentleman with graying hair and a kind face comes to visit us in his dinghy. He asks discreetly: "Do you want to do any shopping with your baby? I can take you if you like. My car is at the club."

Russ is so kind that we accept at once. He stops at the club for a minute to telephone. A few minutes later we are in a large American store in the Canal Zone, where everything is much cheaper than in Panama. We write down the price of everything we are interested in in a notebook. We are not allowed to buy anything here. You have to have a Canal Zone resident's card, but Russ will buy them for us. Russ gets some fresh food for us now to eat this week. Then he asks, almost timidly: "Are you in a hurry? Do you have something fixed for this evening? If not, I'd love you to meet my wife, Polly."

We accept again, and ten minutes later Laurence is stroking some thick green velvet chair covers. She puts her cheek against the material and smiles—it's soft. She seems amazed at this new world that doesn't move. She opens her eyes wide in her little bald head, and Russ christens her "Big Big Black Eyes." Polly and Russ have the serenity of a couple who have lived their lives to the full. They also seem extremely young although they have numerous grandchildren. They sail and fish and their holidays are very adventurous for a leading canal official. Polly asks us to share a simple dinner. This civilized existence is very refreshing after our stormy crossing.

Another advantage of civilization. For 2.50 francs, which I put in the club washing machine, I can wash sixteen pounds of clothes —everything we have. Meanwhile, Christian is bargaining in Panama. He comes back with a good radio and a guitar. Cigarettes are only seventeen centimes a pack. At about eleven, Russ and Polly take us in their speedboat to Toboga, a very attractive little tourist island, which has managed to keep its primitive character. The pineapples there are delicious and cheap.

Next day, taking advantage of the low tide, we moor alongside a wrecked cargo boat on the bank opposite Balboa, at the other end of the famous Panama Bridge. The tide goes down more than six feet. We take up our scrapers, brushes, scouring powder, minium, paint and anti-fouling once more, the last with no great confidence. By seven we've finished and the tide has turned. As it gets dark we suddenly find we're itching all over.

"Nonos!"

It's too late to take cover: they must have surreptitiously injected their poison into us as soon as the sun went down. They are little midges that you can hardly see, and that seem much more venomous here than in Polynesia.

Laurence? I go aboard at once, but by some miracle she seems to have escaped. We hastily swallow some insect-bite pills and use up two tubes of insect repellant in the night. At about 1 A.M., in broad moonlight, we leave the wreck with no regrets.

Christian spends the remaining time making up a list of useful provisions to take with us. I go on foot to Balboa with Laurence every day; and she chatters away in her stroller. I pick up *atoni* mangoes from the beautifully kept grass along the roadside, just fallen off the trees and deliciously ripe. Laurence loves them and I'm delighted to be able to introduce her to trees, leaves, grass.

Balboa is clean, tidy, prefabricated, immensely well kept and hygienic. Shops and cars are air-conditioned and dogs don't foul the streets. In Panama City on the other hand complete squalor and total poverty go cheek by jowl with sickening wealth and the utmost dishonesty. Panama has its own smell, which is heavy, overperfumed or fetid, humid and suffocating, bigoted and depraved. By a shop selling plastic religious souvenirs an urchin of twelve slides up to you to offer his fourteen-year-old sister for a dollar.

Panama—slums, stolen passports, duty-free shops where people haggle over the last penny. In some streets you shiver and get the feeling you are surrounded by murderers. Not necessarily mean, dark streets. Streets with smart apartments, and villas with gardens surrounded by high, wire fences, where it is deathly silent even in the daytime. There's no one about and murder is no illusion: there's one every day. Panama is in a state of semi-permanent revolution. At present, for instance, the Americans from the Canal Zone don't care go there for fear of being gunned down.

We are supposed to be leaving tomorrow. Some friends are getting in the provisions for us. We take care of water, fuel, kerosene; sugar, flour, potatoes, onions, all in forty-pound sacks. We wonder how we'll get it all in the lockers. When we arrive on board at four o'clock, we are surprised to find a large case of provisions we've ordered, plus all sorts of presents: little jars of food for Laurence, packets of cigarettes, cookies, and chocolate. With a note from Mr. and Mrs. H., whom we have met only briefly once or twice: "When our children go to Europe this summer, many people whom we will perhaps never meet will give them a helping hand, in one way or another. This is our way of thanking them." We are very touched, and sad not to be able to see them again to try to tell them how grateful we are.

The next day, Sunday, Russ asks us to accept a case of presents: fifty little jars for Laurence, rusks—and for us detachable stainless-steel heads for the underwater guns, cartridges for our twenty-two LR rifles, cigarettes, an enormous bag of candy, and at the bottom of the case a twenty-dollar note, "in case you need it in the Galápagos."

But we still haven't got a visa.

We go back to the blasted Ecuadorian consul, who still wants $17. We have to leave because our time is up. But we are a bit worried because on May 27 the headlines in the leading American newspapers read: "CIVIL WAR IN FRANCE. Eight million strikers in the streets of Paris. Paris is besieged by students and Communists. Paris is dead. Everything has come to a standstill." It's very upsetting when one can't do anything about it. What is "duty"? What possibilities are open to us? Not many. It would be at least a year before we could get back to France. Will Didier and Christian be called up? We feel there is nothing we can do except continue on our way to Tahiti, and see there what we can do. But we're worried about our family and friends who are besieged in Paris. I can't help thinking about all the horrors of war, which my parents often described to me, and which still haunt my nightmares.

We go to see Fergusson on the *Serena*. Fergusson is a law unto himself: every year he spends several weeks' holiday on the canals of Patagonia and Tierra del Fuego. He insists that the fantastic beauty of the scenery makes it worth the effort. He makes us want to see it for ourselves. He gives us sixty feet of best-quality nylon rope, and some very supple Terylene cloth to patch our sails with.

At nine-forty-five, after a last communal shower in soft water by the yacht club landing stage, we set sail into the Pacific.

At ten-forty-five, Russ joins us in his motorboat: he's brought Polly and a young couple. We leave the *Alpha* in the care of the self-steering gear and all go aboard his boat. It's most impressive seeing one's yacht sailing along with no one on board. A phantom boat. Russ takes the young couple, who are learning to sail, aboard the *Alpha*. And we continue like this all day, one behind the other. Sometimes we go ahead of the yacht so we can see it sailing up toward us or from the side. Then at last it's time for Russ to go back, before the sun sets. He leaves us with an icebox full of milk shakes, frozen chicken, butter, Coca-Cola, beer—and he has tears in his eyes when he says goodbye to Big Big Black Eyes, who can't stop smiling at him. We feel tearful too.

One day passes, then another. The wind is very feeble and from the south—and it's the south we're heading for. We're making no progress and it never stops raining. None of us dares say what we are thinking: the doldrums.

We are at the end of the period of favorable winds, and consult our manuals. Most navigators take ten days to a fortnight to reach the Galápagos. They go south more or less along the coast of South America.

We are still only a few miles from Panama, becalmed in the Gulf. But we can get the Washington speaking-clock on our new radio and it gives the time every five minutes throughout the day and night. Modern technology is really amazing. We could determine the boat's position with an ordinary alarm clock.

All the fresh food spoils very quickly in this heat: pineapples, avocados, bananas, tomatoes, peppers ripen in three days. So we try to catch a turtle to console ourselves—with no success. We also lose a dorado, which gets off the hook at the last minute.

Everything in cardboard packets—Laurence's cereals, porridge, semolina—gets damp. One should have everything in hermetically sealed cans with desiccator bags. But eggs coated with Vaseline will keep several weeks if they are fresh to start with.

We are hardly moving at all, and we don't man the tiller. It should be peaceful—but the annoying thing is that our living space is so reduced. The forecastle is taken up by Didier and the vegetables. The washroom is stuffed with provisions and is unusable. The cockpit is unbearable in this heat with the burning sun. Which leaves the saloon. Laurence takes up the whole of my bunk: there is only the skipper's to sit on. We can sit or lie down on it and that's about it.

It's hardly believable! here we are, three adults, plus a baby who is beginning to climb everywhere, which cramps us even more because we have to be careful all the time not to trip or fall over her. She's seven months old and can climb out of the cabin by herself, even at sea with the boat rocking. The exit ladder is a vertical plank about three feet high with two little steps fixed across it. Laurence pulls herself up by her arms and installs herself flat out on top of the engine to sleep like a kitten, choosing the most stable part of the boat.

It's extremely difficult for two or three people to be cooped up together day and night on a very small boat. The lack of privacy is unbearable for a woman. It is terrible never to be able to be by oneself, and even if there is a curtain or door as a physical barrier between me and the others for a minute, everyone is aware of every detail of my toilet. It is rather like an indecent assault going on for months on end. And Christian and I fight frequently, our nerves taut. A voyage isn't exciting and intoxicating every day. You have to weather a lot of blows before you can enjoy a nice beach or a superb sunset. But I think it would be unbearable to live ashore with a husband who goes off at seven in the morning and comes back at seven at night, exhausted by his day's work and having spent the best part of the day with other people, doing things I can't take part in.

I still think that love is the pleasure one shares in being alive, having a roof over one's head, not suffering from the cold or hunger, having a child you bring up together. Above all sharing the same risks permanently. In modern life we don't share the same risks any more.

It's raining and there's not a breath of wind. A shoal of tuna fish swim round the *Alpha,* which is trailing along no faster than the current. Some bonitos pay us a visit. The weather is torrid and humid and we think longingly of the trade winds. The washing never dries: even when it isn't raining the air is too damp.

Suddenly, at about ten o'clock, I see Christian creep down to get his harpoon with the detachable head. He comes quietly back on deck, with a strong bit of rope. Didier takes the rope without saying anything. And—they've got it. The detachable head has gone into the only soft part of the turtle, in its neck. An ordinary tip would have gotten twisted. Christian tows the turtle, which gives Didier time to pass a line around it. A few minutes later the beautiful green-backed creature is on deck: it must have been incautious enough to take a nap floating on top of the water.

We have turtle steaks for lunch—lovely thick, red steaks. In the evening a stew with vegetables. As there's no wind and no chores to do, we celebrate. Large old turtles have a strong fishy taste, which can be most unpleasant and put you off them for good. But a young turtle, especially if you have time to purge it in clear water for a few days, can taste of any meat from beef to pork.

The turtle is delicious, but there's a lot of it and it goes on for a bit too long. We've already eaten it four times in two days and there's plenty left. We take our bearings to cheer ourselves up: 220

miles in a fortnight. It's our record for slowness. And there's still no wind, only a cross sea, and we're making no headway, in spite of the engine, in the grilling sun.

Christian harpoons a second turtle. But the turtle gets the better of him, because it goes off with the detachable tip and the nylon gets caught in the engine propeller. And several sharks appear just as he's about to dive down and investigate. As soon as they look as if they're leaving, Christian bravely gets into the water and untangles the nylon line in record time, while I keep a lookout.

We have noticed that porpoises make a sucking noise, like kissing. As soon as we hear it we go on deck and a few minutes later they appear. Laurence recognizes them and is wild with delight to see them leaping and playing only a few feet away from her.

Didier has finished his tobacco. He studies his English with me. Christian is worried. We mend the sails nearly every day and we're making no headway. It's getting desperate. We begin listing everything on board which could be made into sails: old sheets, pareos, and a large tarpaulin.

One day passes, then another. A nice surprise. When we wake up we see Malpelo ahead of us! A fortnight to get to Malpelo; it's incredible. It usually takes three to five days. But let's not celebrate too soon; it's still only on the horizon. The rock, less than halfway between Panama and the Galápagos Islands, is inaccessible and uninhabitable, right in the middle of the sea. It's an important landmark—at least we're on the right track. It must be awful to be stuck there, miles from anywhere, in the doldrums.

It's very chilly and we get out our sweaters and trousers. At this time of year the Humboldt Current brings an icy stream, which the whales love, from Cape Horn. The wind is still fairly strong, still against us.

This morning Malpelo is still ahead of us. We begin to ask ourselves if it's a mirage, a hallucination. It's discouraging going so slowly, especially as the wind is wearing out our sails to no purpose. If it doesn't change, will we go back to Panama or proceed very, very slowly to the Galápagos? There must also be a very strong cross current. The wind changes all the time and it's a real struggle to keep our course.

We gaze in silence at the infernal zigzag route we have been following for over a fortnight. Again our only chart of the Pacific is a pilot chart, which stretches from Australia to South America. We have a chart of the Galápagos and three of the Marquesas Islands. In the evening, when the sun goes down, Malpelo is behind us at last.

Friday, June 14. The *Alpha* is a year old. It's a shame to be in the doldrums for her birthday. We've given up counting the days or the distance still to cover. And where are we going anyway? Will we do three thousand miles at a speed of one or two knots?

What a night. No moon, gigantic waves, and the lugubrious sound of the tiller threatening to break at any moment. The wood is split along almost the entire length. Christian has mended it as best he can with nylon rope, but in this sea the rudder thrashes about and wrenches at the lashed tiller. The waves constantly wash over the bow, and at about 1 A.M. the jib goes. Didier and Christian change it again in the pelting rain. Then it's the mainsail's turn. We furl it for the rest of the night. Our poor skipper can't go to sleep again. He keeps sitting up and then lying down and turning over again, worrying about the sails.

The boat is perpetually submerged, the gunwale under water. But the *Alpha* rides gracefully up and over the great waves, and sometimes breaks through the crests or goes under. She's too heavy, weighed down by barnacles. The sky is still gray, menacing; we've had enough of this weather. Why don't we call in at Cocos? That would break the voyage for us.

8

Our Own Island

The sea is making an incredible din. A sound of tumultuous torrents. Currents are eddying in every direction, like great rivers crashing into each other all round us.

But life goes on much as usual in the cabin, as if we were in harbor. Christian writes; we are rather like shipwrecked mariners but we must keep up an appearance of normality. I force myself to keep the boat clean. Our life is organized down to the last detail as usual. It's vital not to let ourselves go. English lessons with Didier are important for keeping up morale. It's important to learn and work at something, to nourish our brains, which have no outside stimuli. We're like caged animals at the zoo. And we don't even have people staring at us to distract us—I gaze in horror at the tracks the weevils have made in the rice, semolina, pasta, and porridge. Laurence is entranced by the little holes running through the dried peas. Christian is staring at a spot no bigger than a pinhead on our pilot chart of the Pacific—Cocos Island. We've decided to call in there.

The dead calm continues endlessly. *Doldrums,* notes the skipper. We've said it now. The weather doesn't correspond with the true definition of the term, since "doldrums" means an area without any wind at all. But a contrary wind, powerful currents, and calms in succession have just about the same effect on us. Twenty miles a day, for weeks on end, is quite something.

We don't say "When we get to" now, but "If we get to Cocos Island." Each object on board has taken on vital significance. We can't waste or lose anything. We have to economize on writing paper, the soft eraser for the charts, the kerosene for lights and cooking; we mustn't lose pencils or cooking things; we have to count our provisions. We won't be able to buy anything for a long time.

Fishing for dorados continues, and we always eat them raw. All our clothes and bedding dry in the sun, thanks to the calm weather. The water we shipped two days ago has made everything damp and there's a smell of mildew everywhere. Christian estimates our position exactly, which puts us back at a point behind our yesterday's position, but we hadn't taken astronomical bearings for a week since we were covering so few miles a day.

Three o'clock. Christian suddenly leaps up: a large object has jolted roughly against the stern on the starboard side. There's a second heavy scratching, like the sound of a grater against the barnacles. Only sharks behave like that. There are about a dozen of them, the smallest one at least six feet long. They've come to rub their backs on the hull.

Luckily the whales don't have the same idea. The *Alpha* seems rather low in the water when one thinks about all those sharks, and remembers how far they can leap after their prey when necessary. It makes our flesh creep.

Sometimes I think we're completely mad to let ourselves be buffeted like this all day and all night. Shipping water over the side; being glued to the helm. But it's less depressing than having to get up at dawn in an icy fog, going to work on a subway—a better way

104

I think than spending your life in a badly lit and stuffy office, where everyone nurses their grievances in communal misery.

Having grown up in Polynesia, where it was easy to fulfill one's needs without living crammed together and coldly dependent upon one another, I find our large sophisticated cities growing sadly more and more like the human zoo Desmond Morris describes. I feel incapable of voluntarily bringing up children far from the natural world, far from sun, with no sand and water to splash about in.

Disaster has struck tonight. The boat is yawing in the wind, and Christian gets up to put her back on course. But this time there is an awful crack as the skipper swings the sail across to the other side.

"Didier," he shouts hoarsely, "quick, give me a hand."

Didier, roused from a deep sleep by a jerky movement of the *Alpha,* is on deck in a matter of seconds.

"Blast!"

The mainsail is torn right across, in tatters from one end of the boom to the other, by the first reef.

In the hurly-burly, I find myself on deck to inspect the damage just as the skipper lowers the sail. I could weep. The canvas is rotten, swollen with salt and burned by the sun.

We have no spare sail and can go only 150 miles at most with the engine. When we had to choose between twenty-five extra gallons of fuel and twenty-five of drinking water, we didn't hesitate: we chose the water. And we have about five months' supply of foodstuffs on board. But can we hoist our sheets and *pareos?* It's out of the question to mend the sail at sea, because it has to be stretched out flat. As a temporary measure the skipper reefs the sail. The torn part is rolled up and securely fixed to the boom, but the area of sail is greatly reduced. The wind is moderate and the hull is covered with weed, which trails like fins down the sides. When will we get to Cocos?

We've been at sea twenty-six days already. We would possibly have reached the Galápagos long ago if we'd sailed due south, using the engine. There is not much fresh food left. Only a few lemons, a lot of onions, and only a kilo of potatoes. We'll have to

105

eat vitamin pills. We've got enough drinking water for a month. If it rains we can collect some more in Laurence's bath, under the mainsail.

The skipper says we'll reach Cocos tomorrow. There do seem to be more birds and the wind seems a bit stronger; but seabirds can go long distances. We have seen them everywhere, even fifteen hundred miles from the shore. Quite small birds, which have to spend many nights at sea. But today the skipper puts the points of the dividers with one on our position, one on the spot representing Cocos Island. There are fifty miles to go. I can't believe we'll hit it exactly right. We all bend over the chart. Laurence smiles at us, her four baby teeth bright in her little round head.

This little bit of woman takes up all my time. I realize that everything I do or think is qualified by her existence. I need to stand back from her. I sometimes think it must be bad for her always to live with her father and mother; I'm afraid she'll become spoiled or capricious. But so far there's no problem. She smiles and laughs all day long.

At sunrise, we catch a glimpse of the unaccustomed contours of an island in the morning mist off to the southwest. We see a mountain sharply delineated for an instant, then it melts away. Are we imagining that a cloud is an island?

The sun gradually rises behind us. Cocos Island is clearly visible directly ahead—but the wind is no stronger. In the afternoon Christian decides to start the engine so we will get there before nightfall. And then the crank handle snaps. He tries to mend it. The engine won't start. It hasn't been used for too long and is useless. Damn!

No sails, a boat weighed down with provisions and covered with barnacles, a tiller that has to be held at an angle and that doesn't respond properly even then—and now this rotten engine. It's infuriating, being so close to land and so helpless to get there.

By the end of the afternoon it has started to drizzle. The sky gets more and more overcast. At sunset we are one or two miles from shore, but the weather is terrible and we can't land in the dark and mist because we have no charts. We learned later that Cocos Island belongs to Costa Rica. One must have an authorization from that country to go there. To get it you have to promise on your

106

honor not to look for Morgan's treasure. We're only looking for a bit of peace and quiet. We have bad dreams all night, and keep getting up, while Christian tacks out to sea, then back toward land, toward the sea, the land. In the morning it rains more and more, with gusts of wind followed by a dead calm.

A current drives us along the coast. It's tricky without an engine. More than once I think we've foundered as gigantic black rocks tower over us, or the cliff, suddenly all round us. Christian has wisely gotten some empty jerrycans ready, which we can use as a raft to drop anchor out at sea if necessary. Sometimes the current takes us directly toward the cliff. So Didier and Christian paddle with planks six feet long. What a blessing the paddles are, but they're so slow.

At last we're there, we're anchored. We scraped the bottom with the keel and had to pull up the chain and anchor. Finally we dropped our good old CQR successfully in a marvelous sandy bay.

The sun is shining, tinged with the reds and orange of sunset. The colors of the island come alive. We see great scarlet balls in the trees: edible fruit? But the fruit fly off. We were lucky to arrive just at the frigate birds' mating season: to attract the females the males swell out huge red sacks under their necks and beaks.

We inspect the luxuriant vegetation in vain for a last lingering monkey or poisonous snake. There are only the frigate birds, boobies, egrets, and every kind of seabird, as far as the eye can see. They all squawk in unison. The boobies dive straight down as if they had been fired from a gun, with their wings flat against their bodies. They never fly up without a fish in their beaks.

We are about 500 miles to the west of Panama, and 350 miles north of the Galápagos Islands. "Our" little island is about 600 feet high and must be about 15 miles in circumference. The cliffs rise sheer above a deep sea. Beyond the two arms of the bay, bare black rocks rise from the water. It seems difficult to penetrate into the interior of the island. We can see five waterfalls from the deck of the *Alpha*. All that fresh water going to waste. I can feel the water on my salt-dried skin. What is the secret of this deserted island? It is so like Polynesia, with its soft exuberance.

On examining the bay more closely—it is called Chatham Bay —we see a small watercourse that seems to indicate a rift in the mountain. The color of the vegetation, the way the trees grow . . . is it a valley? We're delighted at the idea.

There are dozens of sharks. Are they fonder of human flesh than those of the Tuamotu Archipelago or Bora Bora? As we're uncertain we decide that the "women and children" shall stay on board while the men go and investigate before it gets dark, which will be fairly soon. They load into the inflatable bath: camouflage outfits bought in the Puces market, socks and gloves, anti-mosquito cream for their faces, caps—and the gun. Wearing their bathing trunks, they get into the water in the midst of the sharks' fins. Some small ones come and sniff the bath and the flippers of the two valiant swimmers as they do a frantic crawl to the beach, fifty feet off. Ten minutes later Laurence and I can see them standing correctly dressed on the sand, which seems unreal to me because I've seen nothing but water for a month.

They inspect the beach, scrutinize the trees from which the snakes should writhe—or some nice little monkeys. They are ready to tackle all the dangers promised by the stories about Cocos Island. They dig around and turn over dead leaves and tree trunks looking for red ants or harmful insects. Suddenly Christian raises his gun: at the far end of the beach a goat is staring at him quite unafraid. Our skipper presses the trigger, but he's forgotten to release the safety catch and the goat trots calmly off into the thicket.

The animals on the island must be descendants of those that were brought and abandoned there by the pirates whose lair this was. Tonight at any rate our two hunters will dream of the thousands of oysters they have seen clinging to the rocks at low tide, of egrets, which which should be delicious on a spit, and of the wild pigs squealing on all sides. We are longing to taste fresh meat again.

In fact, this beautiful wilderness, gilded by the last rays of the setting sun, is not at all frightening. One feels that if one has no fear, and lives at its own rhythm, it will be a friendly island.

Laurence doesn't seem interested in the birds that wheel above us with loud cries, but she watches fascinated as the tip of the island is silhouetted darkly against the flaming sky. As always in the Tropics, night falls abruptly twenty minutes after sunset. The incessant chatter of the birds dies away, becomes a whisper, a rustling sound: the silence is filled with intense nighttime activity. There's always a fish leaping, a bird flapping its wings in the branches. The sea rises and falls, taking pebbles with it and murmuring on the beach. We are right in the middle of the calm belts that the sailors of old dreaded, far from all civilization. There are no humans on the island. But there is fantastic animal life—and the air is filled with heavy, exotic sounds.

We spend a peaceful night in the motionless boat. Have a proper meal, at the table, with plates. We get out some clean sheets and Christian and I install ourselves in our cabin in the forecastle. Didier shares the saloon with Laurence.

After our dinner of corned beef with rice and onions, we sit on deck and the captain plays some flamenco on his guitar. We finish the evening with lingering Tahitian melodies, which die away into the night. Then, in the silence, the nocturnal rustling becomes an uproar. When I was a child this humming both fascinated and upset me. I forced myself to dissect what grownups called silence. But it rapidly gave me a kind of vertigo, a feeling of a bottomless precipice. So I would pick up a little sand and tell myself quietly that the night was exactly the same as the daytime, but without any sun. And yet the night is quite a different world.

Toward midnight, a heavy bump wakes us up abruptly from a deep sleep. Then silence. Then another bump. We've run aground. As the tide is very low and must be about to turn, the skipper decides to wait for high tide to move the *Alpha.*

At six o'clock the first rays of the sun, already blazing and burning hot, turn the cabin into an oven. Luckily the pure brilliant white of the boat beats back the heat: even when the sun is at its height the steel of the deck is cold to the touch. Thanks to that and the good ventilation of the hatches fore and aft, we have always, luckily, had to have bedclothes at night, even in the Tropics. At the first blaze of light, I push the blanket to the end of the bed and Christian opens the hatch. Our two heads bob up from the fore-hatch. We have to half close our eyes in the blinding light. The sea sparkles; it is warm and the water looks lovely. The birds have been awake and out hunting for hours. One will dive down beside us, come up with a fish, be chased by one of its own kind, lose its catch, snatch it back, lose it again—squawking loudly.

Oh, how lovely it would be to dive naked into the clear water.

But it is still full of sharks, of course. Didier and Christian have their first swim while I make some biscuits with flour, oil, baking powder, and water. I use a glass to press the dough flat, and for an oven, put an aluminum plate upside down on the Primus, with the frying pan on top covered with a saucepan. The boys are swimming round the *Alpha.* The fish seem never to have met human predators before, invading their lagoon. They come sniffing round the two strangers. A shark with a long dorsal fin and a tail with white marks on it brushes past the tip of Christian's gun. A few yards father on, some scad come leaping with a flash of silver from water thrashed into a whirlpool by the sharks. I call the others back for breakfast. The biscuits are a bit hard on the teeth but taste delicious after our diet of stale or moldy, green bread, followed by rice with powdered milk, then rice with water and jam.

We free the anchor from the coral it has gotten caught in and make our way between the clusters of coral with our makeshift paddles to a deeper anchorage. This will mean there is farther to swim, through the sharks, to get ashore.

The sun is getting higher and it's time to think about some food. The fishermen can take their choice from the vast aquarium of fish of every color and kind. I place my order: "A sole for Laurence and two red mullets for me."

Christian will probably bring back two or three large scad for himself, and Didier some groupers. Fifteen minutes later I have cleaned and scaled them and they're sizzling in the pan. The sharks are fighting over the entrails nearby.

After our surfeit of dorados and turtle meat, we really appreciate these small inshore fish, with their delicious tender flesh. There is no oil or mud or sewage here. How has Laurence managed not to swallow a bone? She hasn't made any fuss, at any rate. She's now eight months old.

This afternoon I can enjoy putting up a line to hang my washing on. The sheets, towels, and diapers stretch from stay to shroud and are drenched with sun as they flap in the wind. There's nothing nicer than sleeping on a sheet dried in the sun after a month of a damp sleeping bag soaked in sea water. While I'm enjoying this very basic and prosaic pleasure, Laurence is discovering math. She's busy passing three rings on a chain from one hand to the other, in different ways that help her to appreciate space and distances.

Her favorite pastime is carefully and conscientiously collecting everything that doesn't get swept up each day: grains of rice from a crack in the floor, crumbs, hair, down—which she unfortunately puts in her mouth. As I am trying to forestall her with a damp sponge, on all fours, under her indignant eyes, there's a loud rapping on the grating of the cockpit. A moray nearly three yards long is thrashing about frantically on deck, its tail beating against the seats like a whip. Its skin is dark brown and amber colored. It opens its jaws fiercely, revealing sharp teeth, and the round, menacing eyes in the smooth, shiny head are obviously looking for a prey. It rears its neck up like a snake and makes for anything that moves. It's quite the finest moray Christian and Didier have ever caught. This one could easily bite through a wrist. Its savage and evil expression looks truly prehistoric.

Perched on the engine canopy, Laurence watches it. As the great mouth snaps in her direction, she gives a nervous cry and then laughs. She has the confident air of a baby who knows she is safe and points her chubby little finger at the "thing"—which will make a tasty soup, a West Indian *blaf,* and some delicious steaks grilled over a brazier.

My two savages get into the water to attack the barnacles with a scraper. The "scratch, scratch" resounds through the hull. Fish appear on all sides, not in the least afraid of these intruders from another world. They come and sniff the humans and gobble up the shells from the *Alpha*'s belly in passing. And suddenly, miraculously, dozens of them rush at the hull and snatch greedily at the barnacles. From inside the boat one can hear little scratching sounds, which get louder and louder, coming from all directions. Didier and Christian watch the underwater feast for a while entranced and then come up, delighted to be able to throw away their scrapers. It's a nasty job underwater. And the fish go on feasting all night, while we dream of a smooth, clean hull, gliding soundlessly through the transparent water.

How lovely to be here on our own island.

The underwater fishing recommences. When Christian has caught his first fish, a little grouper comes up to him and he gives it a bit of his catch. The grouper gobbles it up. After that it obviously feels it has been adopted and follows its new friend every-where, like Jojo the Grouper in Captain Cousteau's film. It's there when Christian dives down from the boat, waiting for its little bit of fish. It would be his faithful companion for nineteen days.

Our skipper is amazed that his childhood dreams should have come true like this. Robinson Crusoe's desert island, Cousteau's *Silent World*—and with his little family beside him.

"It is good to be able to realize one's dream," he writes tonight. *"It's even better if one can realize it without sacrificing family life."*

We feel free because we've followed our choice to the end. We could have made a soft city life for ourselves, with running water, a shower, electricity. We could have taken out all kinds of insurance policies, against sickness, injury, and death, and installed ourselves in comfort and security, which are certainly greatly to be valued. We could have been content with our dreams as we walked hand in hand along the quays, thinking of wonderful voyages, and quietly envying those who had the "luck" to be able to go on them. We could have been satisfied with what others had shown us in books or in films.

But we knew that you can't describe a ray of sunlight. That beauty, like happiness, is untranslatable. Poets spend their lives trying to describe the emotion they feel, an emotion that cannot be grasped because it is human, living, ever changing.

We felt confusedly that only an adventure we had lived could satisfy us, excite us. It wouldn't be easy to achieve it. We had to work hard for months on end to buy our boat. And afterward our life was a battle with nature that cost us continual effort. We knew no one would give us encouragement or help us. "It wasn't a sensible thing to do." The kindest would merely smile gently, incredulously. But we would live our dream together. And today here we are, experiencing our adventure, on this desert island. An intense excitement pounds through our veins. Our bodies are in-tensely aware. The sun licks us with its warm caresses, enfolds us. Our eyes aren't large enough to bear all this light. Our ears are alert, our eyes rove ceaselessly, our nostrils quiver at strange scents. The morning of the third day dawns.

We went to bed with the sun and rise with it. As soon as it's light Christian takes apart our bilge pump, which we bought in

112

Cannes. It's a ten-franc pump, and gets blocked all the time. Luckily we don't have to bail out more than a couple of gallons of water every two months. As on all boats, the pump through the stern near the engine.

While I'm scrubbing the deckhead, where the kerosene lamps have left a gray sediment, Christian fixes an extension to the bilge pump, intending to pump up the twenty gallons of diesel oil that he put in a reserve tank. He starts pumping, but only water comes up. We all remember the oil that made the afterdeck slippery on the port side of the boat when the boat listed as we left Panama. We thought there was a tiny leak, a few drops escaping from the join between the deck and one of the cockpit backboards. The whole twenty gallons has been gradually replaced by sea water, as diesel oil is lighter than water. Christian stops up the hole with cement and empties the tank. That will mean less weight to carry —but also less diesel oil, our only reserve supply. There's only the ordinary tank, which holds ten gallons—that is twenty hours at six knots, or 120 miles.

When the *Alpha* is clean and tidy, we start mending the sails. The most difficult part is sewing on a patch almost the length of the mainsail boom. The tear isn't very straight, and also the terylene sail is a bit misshapen and stretched, so that it's impossible to mend it without making pleats that will make it weaker than ever. And to make it worse the two pieces are very frayed. We use the triangular needles, which cut through the threads of the material. But what else could one use to get through five layers of stiff terylene, hardened by salt and sun? We push with all our might, using a sailmaker's palm. The needle is pulled out with pliers on the other side.

After three hours of this work in the grueling sun, we all dive into the water. And, while the two fishermen go off, followed by their little grouper, which now always accompanies them, I sit on a clump of coral, convoluted like a brain and the color of pale honey. Here and there in the crevices, the "jaws" of clams—red, green, blue, sulfur-colored, phosphorescent—open and shut. I sit there without moving. In a few minutes I'm surrounded by fish. First come tiny luminous blue ones, each with a black stripe down its back. They must be about an inch long. They have come out from under the coral reef, spreading out in a cloud, and swim

113

around my legs in a shoal, without touching me, but razor close. They have a good look, inspect me thoroughly, then return to browse under the coral. I can hear the sound they make quite clearly. Then come flat, oval fish, luminous yellow, with wide black stripes. They are about six inches long, and come from another clump of coral. They too swim round me, opening their mouths just by my legs as if they wanted to taste them, but without touching me or brushing against me. Two gleaming scad do a somersault. A grouper almost touches my mask, stops and looks at me and then swims away. Then I see two little sharks about a yard long, motionless on the surface, watching me. I beat at the water to drive them away, and make for the beach. As I stand up in the water after taking off my flippers, I feel something rub against my right ankle, and turn round to see three fins scudding out to sea. Those damn sharks aren't afraid of anything.

Happiness at sea. It's an indescribable pleasure to feel one's bare feet on sand again, after the long, weary weeks when we felt we might never get here. Deep down inside us, in spite of all the experience of those who have gone before, in spite of the fantastic progress made in navigation, each crossing seems like a gamble. On the one hand, in these days of progress, it seems quite natural to be transported from one side of the world to the other. On the other hand one feels almost astonished to be alive and well, and on dry land, at the other side of the ocean.

The sun is already high and Christian is waving a superb crayfish. The skipper reports that he aimed at two young sharks but the arrow slid off their hard skin. He also encountered a fine thornback. Didier brings back some groupers. It's sad we can't take any underwater photographs.

We've been at Cocos Island for four days now. On land there's no need to navigate, but the first few days the skipper automatically made a time check three times a day. Gradually, however, because hunting for food often takes hours, we have forgotten about time. Our automatic watch has stopped because it hasn't been worn. In any case we've taken the time from the sun for a year now, because the watch only shows Greenwich Mean Time. Soon we've forgotten the date too, and wonder how we ever knew what day of the

114

week it was. The sun wakes us every day at six and sets at six in the evening.

For the present we're living from day to day, as if each day were the last we will spend on the island. We're taking as much advantage as we can of this place—but are ready to leave on short notice. At the same time we're making plans to build a log cabin and stay here six months.

It would be ideal if we could lay up the boat and if we had some vegetables to sow. We could be picking tomatoes in less than three months. My Polynesian childhood comes flooding back to me. We've got matches, firearms, and enough food to give us time to discover what there is to eat on the island. There's plenty of fresh water, game, fish, and almonds. But wouldn't Laurence need cereals? Another difficulty is the family would worry when they didn't get news. It's a pity we're not absolutely free.

Our daily life is much like everyone else's, with eating our chief preoccupation. We fish, hunt, scavenge, in a manner worthy of our ancestors. But they were tougher. They say that my grandmother went to the market in Nouméa every week on horseback, riding the ten miles from their plantation. One day when she was in the final weeks of pregnancy she set off on her horse, went to the market, had her child, and rode back the same day with her baby and the things she had bought. I feel very feeble in comparison with such an indomitable figure. And yet she was by no means uncivilized. She knew how to make lace and taught her children to write, read, do arithmetic, history, and geography. She knew the medicinal properties of plants and all about birds. A little of this lore has come down to me via my mother and is invaluable to me.

There must be many edible plants on the island, but which are they? When should they be eaten and how cooked? People who know that taro corms can be eaten and try them raw without cleaning them in running water get a nasty shock. Taro corms contain a kind of tiny crystal that pricks like needles. It's essential to know they dissolve in water. And anyone who has been unlucky enough to taste a green olive from a tree will understand the problem we're faced with. Besides which, if you make a mistake about a plant or fruit you can end up dead.

No supermarkets here. No steak in cellophane, no frozen

vegetables. The meat is still leaping over the mountainside. The almonds—*auteraa*—have a very thick, tough shell. You have to hit them hard between two stones to crack them, taking care not to hit your fingers. Cracking *auteraa* by the roadside on the way back from school was one of my favorite childhood occupations. If the fruit were still ripe, with their lovely plump red skins, my stained hands and clothes earned me a spanking. But the little kernels extracted with so much care were so good that I couldn't resist the temptation.

On Cocos there is no fishmonger to clean, scale, and skin fish. Your fingers get pricked and sometimes your hands cut because scales can be razor sharp. These fish are used to swimming about among the sharks, and are a far cry from frozen haddock fillets. They taste different too.

Then you have to cook all this food. You collect wood and puff at the fire. It all takes time and patience, and then you have to start all over again for another meal. It's impossible to put on fat. You eat enough for ten people and stay thin.

The natural life becomes very exhausting when you're not used to it. But life on board ship is a good preparation for it. It's a revelation to Didier. For me, it brings back memories of the *faré himaa*, the hut apart from the house that was the kitchen—the smell of smoke wafting toward the sea as we came home from school, followed by the smell of coffee or tea with a little coconut milk. You dipped bread with apricot jam or canned butter in it, and that was supper. Then it got dark. There was no electricity. The more determined children studied by the light of a kerosene lamp. Others waited till morning. As soon as it got light you heard children chanting their multiplication tables or their history homework at the tops of their voices.

But I can remember all the household chores this "natural" life involved. If you do everything yourself, you soon find there's very little time left over for anything except sheer survival. After a day like that you need rest. And we have some of the advantages of civilization. We've got harpoons and guns, matches. In the old days Polynesians, who had no flints or sulfur, made fire by rubbing two specially shaped bits of wood together, one convex and the other concave. For hours on end. One can understand why the guardian

116

of the queen's fire was sacrificed if he let the flame go out.

Why do we like this life so much? Perhaps like children who are told "don't do this, don't do that, you're too small, you'll hurt yourself, you're doing it wrong" we're happy to be able to do anything we like without anyone's stopping us. Perhaps too, to be fulfilled, men need to make something with their hands. Apart from a select few who have chosen a trade that allows them to be creative every day, people work to make money, thinking more about the profit they'll get from their work than about what the work demands from them. Work like this, entailing no initiative or sense of responsibility, is incomplete, an uninspired link in a chain of which the workers are not even aware, and no longer satisfies people. It is good to start from scratch and make something completely—which is why craftsmanship is so satisfying. The worker on an assembly line needs a lot of imagination to get any pleasure from his work.

Hunting a wild boar, cutting it up, cooking and eating it are highly satisfying. This is the first time we've really been hunting, in the true sense of the word. The animals are completely free, in every way, because they've never seen men or guns. It's a law of life that one has to kill to eat. Whether it's a plant or an animal, one is forever taking the life of something that only asked to be allowed to live for as long as possible.

There's plenty of game on Cocos Island: wild pigs with long snouts, chestnut skin, and two tusks; short-haired goats; countless birds of every kind. Animal noises, especially from the boars, resound all day long. You see the feathers of large birds, no doubt eaten by the pigs, on the paths the animals make. We already have our hunting ritual: hunting kit, boots, and guns are put in Laurence's bath and floated ashore, through the sharks. This has to be done at low tide. The beach stretches far out then, and you can get a good way around the island without a tedious climb. Then the hunters start climbing, cutting out their path with a machete. After three hours' hard work they reach a plateau, which forms the most extensive part of the island. Animal paths run across it in every direction: the earth is sometimes churned over and ploughed up over several square yards. The vegetation is equatorial, with virgin forest. Giant vines fall from great corkwood trees. The dark undergrowth is

117

covered with damp green foliage. When you turn over the warm leaf mold with your foot, a large cockroach or shiny centipede glides away. There are a few mosquitoes, but no giant ones. Birds make a wild squawking in the palm trees. The sun can't penetrate the thick foliage and you are blinded when you emerge into the light once more. Your feet, unused to shoes, and in spite of thick woolen socks, get covered with blisters from all the walking and climbing, and the blisters then burst and leave your skin raw.

But it's a real joy after a month at sea to be on this plateau surrounded by greenery and animal life. How lovely the damp earth smells. Beside a stream the skipper finds a very old bottle of green blown glass. Perhaps from the days of the great navigators, of Spanish galleons. Very exciting.

An expedition to the interior of the island takes all day. Coming back, when the tide is up, is dangerous. You climb down holding on to the vines or using the rope that the skipper had the foresight to bring. However, the day's excursion doesn't result in any game—and it would be difficult to get down the cliff carrying a dead animal anyway. But at the last moment, only one hundred yards from where the expedition began, a sow and two piglets come to drink at the stream. The hunters take aim—and the animal is cut up on the spot; they get back with four joints of suckling pig. While the pig is being cut up, clouds of flies suddenly appear from nowhere. The meat has to be hurriedly stuffed into gunny sacks.

Four joints: four meals. We are longing to taste the red meat.

We decide it's no good going to the interior of the island for hunting. The best and simplest way is to hide in the long grass by one of the many streams near the shore. The animals come there to drink throughout the day; you only have to decide what size and shape you want. In nineteen days we've killed seven animals. We try to preserve the last one—which is quite an experience. I've never preserved meat and have no book to tell me how, except the pressure cooker book, which says you need preserving jars, which I don't have. But I have some little baby-food jars with screw tops; they are sealed with a synthetic band, which seems as good as new. I cut off some of the best meat and cook it for an hour in the pressure cooker with a little water, salt, and pepper. I wash the pots in salt water but don't sterilize them. I push the meat down well, add a little gravy, and put on the lids, then put them into the pressure cooker with a little water, and heat them for fifteen minutes. When I take them out the tops are blown out, which is quite normal. But when they've cooled down, if they still have raised lids, it means they are bad.

The little jars hold an amazing amount: I got a whole pig into twenty of them. And they lasted over eight months. They might have lasted longer, but we finished them, after eight months, in Tahiti. The meat tastes much nicer than corned beef, and will enable us to vary our menu after ten or twelve days of dorado.

Even on Cocos Island fish is often on the menu. From choice rather than necessity. If you don't mind swimming through sharks it's an underwater fisherman's paradise. Didier and Christian always bring back far too much.

We eat on the spot some of the many thousands of oysters clinging to the rocks. There are also hundreds of dark gray crabs. They're quite unafraid and you can get close enough to them to give them a sharp tap on the back with a stick—and pop them into the saucepan. We fill the pan with them and steam them in salt water; they're delicious.

The rivers are full of crayfish. We catch some with our hands but don't have the right equipment. In Polynesia they have two different methods of catching them. The quickest—the classical method—is to use a little harpoon made of a thin lemon-tree branch with iron darts. You go upriver at night with a Coleman lantern, which blinds the crayfish, and spear them one by one. The other method, which children use, takes time and patience. You take the rib of a coconut leaf foliole, a brown stalk about a yard long that is very thin and supple, but quite strong. Then you get a length of fiber about eight inches long from the coconut husk and make a little rigid lasso which is fixed to the end of the stalk. Then you crouch silently at the water's edge and try to tickle the end of the crayfish's tail. When it's frightened, it leaps back and is caught in the lasso, which tightens round it. You pull it up and begin again. My sister and I spent hours fishing like this when we were children.

Laurence drinks out of a glass, and likes picking up her food by herself, in her fingers. She eats a little of everything. Instead of using a bib, she eats with nothing on. I pop her in the water after she's eaten if she needs a washing. She crawls around and tastes everything: sand, dead leaves, grass, and the moss on stones from the river, which she particularly likes. I'm often horrified to see a centipede fifteen inches long under the damp leaf mold, but I don't let Laurence crawl there.

Her favorite toys are hermit crabs. She follows these funny little creatures, which live in shells abandoned by other animals, seizes the shell delightedly, and is then puzzled to see the crab has disappeared. She scratches at them with her fingers, but it's no good. The little crab has curled up and shut his home with his flattened claws. Though attractive, these little things can pinch hard. You can use them, without their claws, as fishing bait. When you arrive on a beach, the sound of footsteps drives them into their shells, but if you stand still and whistle softly they come out one by one.

The beach, this whole island, is a joy. We have marvelous cold showers under the waterfalls and drink our fill from the springs. All the meat, fish, almonds, fresh water make us forget more sophisticated pleasures. So we are keeping the carton of cigarettes Russ gave us to barter in the Galápagos or elsewhere. We've only got $20 and three bottles of rum, and Tahiti is a long way off. The skipper notes that if we manage to reach the Galápagos we'll be saved because the trade winds will carry us toward Tahiti. If not? Well, if we have to stay on Cocos Island we can always do what our ancestors did and cut the *Alpha*'s name and the date when we arrived into the rock. You see the names and dates of sailing boats on gigantic boulders: 1673, 1740, 1863. We too must seem like Robinson Crusoes to these stones.

July 1. We decide to fill up with fresh water. But how can we transport 125 gallons of water in an inflatable bath? The easiest way would be to get as close to the source of supply as possible, i.e., to the beach. We could then carry it in jerrycans. Also, with the boat hauled up on the beach we could give the hull a lick of paint. No sooner said than done. As soon as we wake up, at high tide, we draw the *Alpha* up on the beach with her keel in the sand, one anchor out at sea and one on land. It's marvelous to be able to go ashore without getting our feet wet. As the tide goes out the *Alpha* is left

120

lying on the sand. So we can only put thirty-five gallons of water in the tank that is in the keel. However, we seize the opportunity of painting the starboard side of the hull. We will wait until the tide is high again at six to take her out to sea and meanwhile have a boar roast over a fire for dinner.

While we're sitting around the fire we suddenly see a fishing boat, which looks as though it's putting out its net. It must be from Ecuador. It's impossible for them not to see the fire and the *Alpha* with her tall mast on the sand. We think up all sorts of deals we can make with the cigarettes and rum. Exchange them for kerosene or rice? We finally decide on kerosene, flour, and sugar. But it's a fantasy. We don't have a dinghy to get out, and it's too far to swim. They seem to have no desire to come and see us. I am indignant: we must look like a shipwrecked boat and they ought at least to come and see. Didier and Christian shout "Hi!" to no avail. As it grows dark they haul up the net and disappear over the horizon, followed by a cloud of birds, which we can hear crying. We haven't seen another human being for over a month.

The tide is up. Operation Launch, and we all go aboard. The *Alpha* clings obstinately to the sand. We start the engine but it's no good. The waves of high tide must have pushed her farther up the sand and she's sunk into it. Christian drops an anchor at sea, secures it with a line to the top of the mast, and tries to make her heel over by pulling with a pulley. If he succeeds in heeling her over enough he will reduce the draft and will be able to work us toward the anchor. But the two men pull in vain, the mast threatens to crack, and nothing happens. We'll have to wait and hope the next tide will come up farther.

At about eight we're all in bed as usual and try to settle down for a good night's sleep. But the *Alpha* begins to bump hard. The tide's going out and the waves are knocking us about. The two men tighten the line to breaking point and try once more to get her to heel over, but with no success. They have great blisters on their hands from pulling on the rope pulleys.

The forecastle becomes unbearable. Christian moves to the quarter berth on the starboard side and I take Laurence to the port berth in the saloon, and she howls each time the keel bumps on the sand. Poor baby. I take her in my arms.

121

Christian is terrified for the mast, but what can we do except wait? When we list the water is forced up the sink, which we immediately shut off. The *Alpha* lists more and more, which gives the waves free rein, and now they're coming in over the tilted cockpit, drenching Christian's and Didier's bunks. I'm on the side opposite the lists and have to keep moving with Laurence. It's awful not to be able to sleep because of the violent jolts. By about eleven-thirty we're on dry sand again. Laurence and I are lying on the bunk board at right angles to the ceiling. I get up in the dark and step on Didier. To get into the cockpit you have to pull yourself up by your arms. It's impossible to use the stove, which isn't on gimbals. At about one-thirty the nightmare starts all over again.

But as the tide comes up the waves are bigger. We have to take in Gigi, who is being knocked around, and shut the door to the cockpit against the waves. The tiller is broken. At four the sea is fairly high and the two men subject their hands to further torture trying to get the *Alpha* off. Instead of tying the line to the top of the mast they tie it at the level of the crosstrees and pull with a series of pulleys. After half an hour's straining, the *Alpha* finally works free.

At last! We really thought we might end our days on Cocos Island. But the engine refuses to start again. We have to creep along in the dark between the coral reefs, using our famous paddles. We finally fall asleep at about six-thirty, exhausted, and wake at midday. It's raining. When it rains we do housework, play Scrabble, baccarat, or dice. Christian always wins at dice and I at baccarat.

The engine is working again. The list of what we have left on board is all too brief: about two quarts of kerosene, some sugar— enough for a week. From July 2 onward it rains from time to time. On the afternoon of the 3rd, after some showers in the morning, the sun comes out at about four while we're playing Scrabble. I suddenly hear a strange squawking and get up and go on deck.

"Christian!"

There's a very peculiar, gigantic object ahead of us, about a dozen yards away. It's like a series of huge trunks floating in a line on the water at regular intervals. Hundreds of birds are perched, clinging, on this shiny black cylindrical object. Each time all the

Laurence takes a bath

Laurence inspects the jib

Christian Guillain

Living on the *Alpha*—just open the doors, and there's the ocean

France and Laurence

Through the Panama Canal

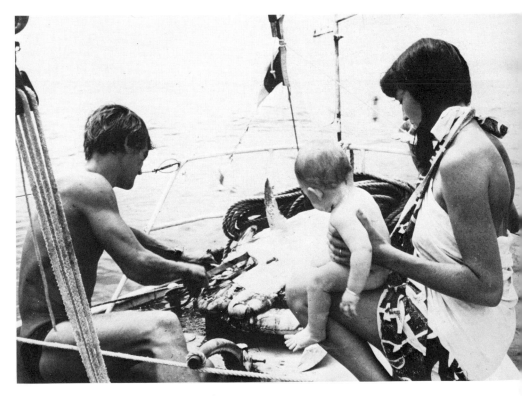

A turtle steak in mid-Pacific

Mending sails

Pygmalion: The floor was easily large enough for three or four couples to dance

Pygmalion stranded at the mouth of the Ebro.
The water around the boat was only ankle deep

In spite of capsizing and going aground, *Pygmalion,*
built with such care, crossed the Atlantic in only eighteen days

Laurence and her wonderful "sea school"

France and Christian Guillain with their three daughters,
Laurence, Mareva and Aïmata. (*J. Violet*)

trunks go under water all the birds fly up, making a great din, and go and perch on the new trunks that appear. We don't doubt for a minute that it's some huge creature, sixty to a hundred feet long. It seems to be like a giant eel in shape, at least a yard in diameter. We can't see its tail or head. How can such a large *thing* get so close to the shore, through the coral reefs? It must take up about a dozen yards of water.

"Shall we go after it?" suggests Didier, delighted at the prospect.

"Count me out," says the skipper, thinking of the monstrous sharks he's seen recently on his underwater fishing trips.

"You're crazy," I add.

How long did it stay there? Ten minutes, an hour? We stood watching it, petrified, and it was with immense relief that we saw it turn toward the entrance to the bay, very slowly, with all the birds perched on top, and clearly silhouetted. If only we could have photographed it. Is Cocos Island, alone and uninhabited in the middle of the Pacific, a refuge where the giants of the sea can emerge?

It rains harder and harder. The rivers turn yellow, then brown, and color the bay. On July 10 in the middle of the afternoon a gust of wind snatches off the forehatch just as a heavy swell gets up. It's enough for us to get our sailing orders. I hurriedly take down my washing lines while Christian starts the engine, and it's goodbye to Cocos Island.

A joint is slowly roasting over the coals on the beach. Another is hanging ready and waiting in a tree. No matter, we'll have to leave them there. We have to go because we don't know what the bay's like in bad weather. It's not very nice leaving only an hour or two before dark, but it's a question of safety. We head for the north of the Galápagos Islands, and don't dare guess how long the crossing will take. But we have to pull on our old salt-stiff sweaters, trousers, and oilskins again, and do balancing feats. We sail round Cocos Island for the last time. There are huge waterfalls everywhere, from the recent heavy rains. Deep valleys and barren ridges follow in succession. There are coconut palms here and there. We are a little disappointed not to have seen more of it. Particularly as we didn't find a single coconut on the island named after them. And green coconuts are so good. We'll come back with nuts and vegetable seeds and plant them here.

The wind is squally and keeps changing direction. The currents have become rapids. But the *Alpha* is clean and makes good progress. The sails are all patched, but they're strongly sewn. Huge swordfish leap in the air by our side. The birds, which are following us, dive-bomb us and Laurence smiles delightedly.

9

A World in Fusion

We adopt our seagoing rhythm once more: sleeping like watchdogs with one eye open, our ears pricked. If this wind continues we'll be at the Galápagos in under a week. We are in excellent humor and so relaxed that Christian is caught off guard.

"Hell! Gigi!"

When Didier reaches the stern, all he can see is a white blob, sinking in the tremendously deep water. Gigi is dead. Gigi has gone, forever. Gigi has been swallowed up and is sinking nine thousand feet or more into the unknown and vasty deeps. Gigi, our best crewmate, our helmsman. Gone to the bottom of the Pacific, taking with her our precious wrench. I saw it topple over just as Didier, who was sitting down, cried out. We shiver, because Gigi is almost human and we subconsciously feel she's part of us: again

125

we are reminded that it is certain death for anyone who falls over-board.

We take watches once more. The two boys do the greater share, but I go on deck from time to time to allow Christian to take our bearings. After their first night on deck the boys seem quite happy. They were getting bored on their bunks, they say. They had finished their supply of reading matter and were reduced to reading the small-print ads. From eight till midnight I keep Christian company, and watch the sea and stars. There are great phosphorescent patches of plankton on the water, and huge phosphorescent fish, which we can't identify. One of them, which seems to be there every night, is at least twenty-four feet long. At the tiller like this, in the cockpit, you realize you're not *on* the sea but *in* it. Sitting on the cockpit seats you can easily lean out and touch the water. If the wind increases in strength, the deck is swamped and you're drenched with icy jets of water. We are *touching* the sea. Laurence also has this very strong impression: a little later, from the deck of a steamer, she would say: "Mummy, I want to touch the sea."

A nice surprise: our position is only 150 miles north of the Galápagos. Ordinarily, we would follow the rules and approach them from the south, at San Cristóbal. It is the same for all ar-chipelagos: each group of islands has a main island where you make your "entry" and present or request a visa from the authorities. However, that being said, it's not always possible to do what you want, when it's a question of wind and wave.

I'm the only one who has any idea what these mysterious islands are like. I have seen some color transparencies of the islands. They are like a desert. Just stones and cacti, and it looks all black. Anne Hervé, who took the slides with her husband, Alain, told me there was nothing on them. "But you should see the colors. The sunsets, the moonlight, the animals. It's very striking. You either love them or hate them," she told me.

Laurence is nearly nine months old. Her hair's beginning to grow—a few blond wisps. She has two upper teeth, which makes six in all. She can get out of the cockpit alone, at sea, which means about a two-foot vertical climb, using arms and legs. It's nice, but it means I have to be even more careful, because there's nothing to stop her falling in the water. Sometimes when I see her perform-

126

ing all these acrobatics I wonder how she'll ever learn to walk. I feel the movement of the boat may retard her in this respect.

We are very near the Equator and will soon be in the southern hemisphere, but it's as cool as spring in the Mediterranean. It's the time of year when the Humboldt Current brings the polar ice from the southern seas. We have to wear our oilskins even in the middle of the day, over sweaters, and mittens, caps, and scarves at night. There are sperm whales swimming in shoals, which is unusual. The great creatures surface all around us. There are some quite a way behind us, and some ahead and to port and starboard. It is frightening when you see them rear up vertically, revealing their great black bodies, their mouths open, complete with enormous teeth, gaping toward the sky. A human would make one mouthful. The terrified dorados huddle round the boat as if seeking protection. The birds, which grow more and more numerous, fight over their prey above us.

We are approaching the first islands in the north of the Galápagos. There are no lights and the currents are numerous, dangerous, and unknown, with only the Wenman rock, directly ahead of us, to land on. We pore over the chart. The skipper indicates the most direct route to San Cristóbal, where we are supposed to go first. The island is right at the other end of the archipelago, going diagonally across it via Santa Cruz, where we have a rendezvous with Bernard on the *Klis*. So we'll make for the latter, passing Isabela on one side or the other. Each island has at least three names—Ecuadorian, English, French—which often bear no resemblance to each other. Isabela is Albemarle; Santa Cruz, Indefatigable; Pinta, Abingdon; Marchena, Bindloe, and so on.

We sail around the rocky cliffs of Wenman. The island is a great plateau of rock 750 feet high, with steep cliffs rising precipitously from the sea, which is very deep there. The vegetation is sparse. It is said to be the place where there are the most species of birds in the world for such a small area. We can see penguins, frigate birds, boobies, albatrosses, petrels. The current is very strong around Wenman, but we sail around it, at a distance of about thirty yards, looking for an anchorage, particularly for a beach or crevice that would enable us to climb up. However, there are only the steep cliffs all around the island, with caves here and there, and

127

the deep ultramarine blue sea below. No goats, apparently. The bird droppings give off a very strong smell.

The morning mist is clearing. At first everything is flat and dark. Then the stone becomes a bluish gray and you can see vertical ridges. Then it changes to pinky gray, and you can see clearly the different layers of rock. Finally it becomes a brown gray, then violet. The birds wheel overhead with great deafening cries, filling the sky. Christian takes in our drag line in case a bird gets caught in it, but it's too late. A booby has bitten the spoon and gotten caught on the hook. We lift it gently on deck to free it. It huddles in the stern, looking defiantly at us, and won't let us touch it. Its great beak could cut a finger in two. The two men finally hold it down and unhook it, and it flies off.

At the foot of the cliffs there are some very dignified little penguins, which stare at us as we go past. A short distance away some turtles, asleep on the surface of the water, dive as we approach. Laurence can see the birds overhead and smiles as she points at them. I attach her harness to the pulpit in the bow, and she watches the sea, so full of turbulent life.

In the morning we find ourselves opposite a lunar landscape, with white rocks and jagged streams of lava. A hellish, burned-out, deserted, raw, volcanic, menacing coast, with no bay or creek where one can shelter for the night. Oh for Cocos Island!

A miraculous catch consoles us a little. The pelicans try to snatch our fish. There are sea lions on the rocks, and they drag themselves heavily along with their strong tails and flippers. The oldest among them, the "grandfathers," remain motionless, keeping a lookout from the highest rocks. These appealing animals are as quick as lightning once they are in the water.

Just as we finish fishing, the sun appears on the horizon and a few rays lighten the overcast sky. It is all suddenly illuminated with fairylike colors. We are transfixed. The island looks immense, warm, beautiful. The black lava, the sea lions—dark violet, gleaming. Half an hour later it's pitch dark. The birds are silent. The sea lions set up their raucous barking, which goes on all night. I hope the anchor holds.

Next day we sail into submerged craters, which form part of the cliffs. It's very strange. We go a few hundred yards up the crater

128

and go about to sail back. In the evening we drop anchor on a huge beach of black sand in Black Bay, just by the strait that separates Isabela and Fernandina, which we reach next day using the engine. Fernandina is just a bare, lifeless cone. At Santa Cruz we learn that less than a month ago it was wooded and had a lake, which was shattered by a volcanic eruption while we were at Cocos Island. We might have seen a last firework display over this volcano that everyone supposed was dead. André de Roy told us later that two seismographers were attacked by a pack of wild dogs there. They instinctively stood back to back—wild dogs are not supposed to attack you from the front. They didn't know how long they stood there. It seemed ages until the dogs went away.

Still the black lava. The scenery doesn't make you want to linger but it does make you want to come back, again and again. It has a slow, magnetic, powerful, irresistible attraction. It is perhaps this that is the charm of the Galápagos, of these heaps of stone.

We'll never forget the crossing to Santa Cruz, to Academy Bay. The strange voyage, carrying on our family life as usual, using up the last of our supplies in our floating capsule, sailing through the frightening lunar landscape. The days passing slowly, the night watches a strain, with a strong wind against us and the dangerous currents and coast all around. None of us sleeps properly. We all want to get away from Isabela as quickly as possible. We are suffering from complete nervous exhaustion, and have just decided to stop at a small island twenty miles ahead, when Didier thinks he sees a port. The skipper takes the binoculars. A miracle. There are a jetty and a few houses. We pass the binoculars from one to the other. Half an hour later we can see the light at the end of the jetty. We prepare for our arrival. Didier sees to the deck while I clean up below. We hoist our quarantine flag and courtesy flag; these are apparently very important in the Galápagos.

At four-fifty we drop anchor. A launch immediately speeds toward us with the local officials on board. Luckily we have arrived before five o'clock, or we would have had to pay the supplementary tariff. An expensive administration, with a base here on Isabela just for two hundred inhabitants—and a few madmen like us.

The officials are charming. The language is a mixture of Indian and Spanish. Sugar is the local currency. You can buy twenty-five packets for a dollar. And twenty-five packets is the price of a live goat, which you can resell in Ecuador for one hundred packets. It seems incredible when you think that they have to walk for over twelve hours up a mountain to get the goats. They hunt them with dogs and catch them alive, as they do the wild cattle. Villamil, the little port we have arrived at, exists only because of the hunting. It was built three years ago and most of the houses are prefabricated. A boat comes once a month from Guayaquil with supplies and to collect the goats and cows. It's due in tomorrow morning. We'll have to wait to get our supplies, because there's nothing left in the village.

At about ten in the morning the *Guayaquil* moors a little way from the port, because the harbor is too small for her. She's a narrow little cargo boat, very high in the water. She rolls dreadfully —you feel sick just looking at her. Boats shuttle to and fro, navigating the dangerous channels, loaded with bricks, cement, wood, kerosene, flour, cans of food. We spend $17 of our remaining $20 on thirty pounds of rice, sugar, some potatoes, five gallons of kerosene, a can of yeast, fifty pounds of flour.

The loading of the goats and wild cattle is a curious and sad procedure. The goats are hoisted up from the launch to the *Guayaquil* with ropes attached to their horns. The cows are the most upsetting. They are too big for the launch and are dragged through the water to the cargo boat. This is done by hauling them by their horns and tail, so that they are lifted out of the sea—otherwise they'd be full of water and no good.

This evening, the Villamil officials have given us a large piece of dried beef, some cocoa, some oat flakes, and lemons. The people are so nice we would like to spend a few days here, and go hunting. But the mooring is very unpleasant, and it would be difficult to get ashore with Laurence. We're still hoping to find a lovely green island. Surely Santa Cruz, with its famous Academy Bay, which everyone visits, must be better than the others.

Santa Cruz. Black lava again, and sea lions, and forests of bare cacti, like sinister candelabra. Then suddenly a marvelous bay with a beautiful white sandy beach—gleaming white. Waves are breaking on a little shoal to starboard, a few miles from shore, but

Christian is irresistibly drawn by the white sand and turquoise water and wants to get closer. As if by some presentiment I fasten Laurence securely, shut all the hatches and shout: "Not so close, Christian!"

And at the same instant an enormous wave gathers under the *Alpha*'s keel and lifts us up. I hold my breath, and stay close to Laurence, who is peacefully asleep. A second breaker passes and thunders down only a few yards away. Christian is concentrating hard at the tiller; Didier is very tense.

A third breaker is gathering by the *Alpha* on the port side, and the seconds seem hours. The green translucent water curls over us as we list—I feel sure it's the end of the voyage for us. The wave swells with a terrible crackling sound and breaks almost directly under the *Alpha*'s keel. I feel weak. We're saved. Didier and I were speechless with fear, and we saw our skipper's legs tremble for the first time.

But the sun's still shining and we reach Academy Bay. The *Klis* is there.

"Wow," says Didier. "If this is what the Galápagos are like— remember Cocos Island?—what the hell are we doing here?"

Bernard Moitessier is on his eighteen-foot trimaran, shouting a welcome through his foghorn at the top of his voice. There are a few other boats there: the *Skaffie* belonging to the young English couple with the kittens; the *Tahiti*. The sea is opaque, rough, angry. The shore is rocky, with only bare cacti as far as the eye can see. The headland, on the side of the bay where we are moored, is dominated by Karl Angermeyer's house—imposing but blending perfectly into the landscape.

In the middle of the bay there are a few other houses—the village. Nearby is the Darwin Station, where a rich American has built a hotel—still empty apparently.

Bernard takes us ashore in his dinghy. "It's the custom on arrival here to have tea with Marga." Marga. A small woman with gray curly hair, bright blue eyes, and slightly overpink cheeks.

We sit in a large room overlooking the sea, around a big table, with the little band of immigrants. They live on the headland, a quarter of an hour from the village by rowboat, or an hour on foot through the cacti. Marga's mother, a lady of eighty, presides over the teapot. The three Angermeyer brothers—Gush, Fritz, and Karl, Marga's husband—sit next to her. Fritz's wife and the de Roy family complete the group. The children aren't there.

This little group live very much on their own, isolated in their ivory tower. They have their own society with its own customs, but no leader, judges, police, or employers. Everyone works and lives for himself. The rule seems to be every man for himself, providing it doesn't harm his neighbor.

The first ones to arrive had difficulty finding good hunting grounds. It sometimes took them months to find a spot regularly frequented by goats, and, once it was found, to find it again with the aid of landmarks or by marking the cacti. Each person has his own hunting ground or grounds and guards its location jealously, especially as the goats are now less numerous and more easily frightened. Until recently the Ecuadorian government gave the immigrants the land they had developed.

They bombard us with questions about our life, our voyage, our plans. We all feel very close, in an expansive mood, and we invite them over to the *Alpha* for 7 P.M. This just gives us time to tidy up a bit and put Laurence to bed. As soon as it's dark, the boat begins to fill up. Gush brings us some carrots, some potatoes from the mainland, and some papayas. There are soon fifteen of us sitting in the *Alpha*'s cabin, as it's cold outside. Christian picks up his guitar, and we all sing. The three Angermeyer brothers have very fine voices, and sing German songs. We all join in, in our own languages. After we've run through our repertory of songs, the skipper lists the various problems we have to tackle: we have to make a new automatic pilot, mend the tiller, careen, and build a makeshift dinghy for our stay here, because the water is icy.

The dinghy: Karl will lend us a corkwood raft. The tiller: there's plenty of strong wood; you only have to cut it. The automatic pilot is more of a problem. There's nothing in the village except cement and bricks. No welding gear, no metal tubing, no plywood. It would take a month to order it from Ecuador: there's only one boat a month and the last one left yesterday. We can't wait that long, because we must cross the Pacific before the hot season, when the trade winds are followed by tropical storms and torrential rain.

132

At 9 P.M., only the de Roys are still there.

"I've got some reinforced concrete," André says. "And an oak plank about one and a half by one yard. We'll see—it ought to be possible, even without welding gear.

A ray of hope.

"Is it true," Christian asks, "that the government pays for every goat killed?"

"It was true until a few years ago. The goats had multiplied to such an extent that they were becoming a danger to the rare fauna and flora of the Galápagos. In particular they ate a very rare plant that was necessary fodder for the famous giant tortoises, which were threatened with extinction. The situation was so grave that the Darwin Station organized mass slaughterings of goats. It was horrible, deplorable. At Barrington, for instance, they killed the animals and left them on the spot. The carcasses slowly rotted in the sun. In the heat the smell was unbearable. The buzzards were bloated and the other goats were frantic. People who depended on hunting for their living gave it up; it revolted you to have to walk through those carcasses. The goats left went far up the mountain. It was months before people could look for new hunting grounds. It's now a day's expedition. You have to leave at five or six in the morning, and walk fast for several hours. You get back just before nightfall."

We're going hunting.

Brrrr—brrrr. 5 A.M. "Brrrr," Christian says, getting up. "The cold and the alarm clock going off so early remind me of setting out for school those gray Paris mornings.

Half asleep, we pull on woolen socks, canvas shoes, trousers, shorts, and sweaters. Laurence is wrapped up snugly and put in her knapsack, on top of her bundle, only her head and arms sticking out. She looks surprised but delighted. Didier and Christian carry guns and gunny sacks.

We all jump on the corkwood raft to go across to the de Roys', who have invited us to breakfast. We have to climb up the *barranco,* the rocky fringe of ancient lava that forms the bay. Some iguanas, startled by this early-morning invasion, scuttle into each other, their hard skins rattling over the rocks. We go round the cacti and take

133

the cliff path leading to a little bay.

The dawn light colors the white sand and exposed twisting roots of the mangrove trees a pinky mauve. Everything is still somnolent, peaceful. There is only a gray heron, standing gracefully on our path, looking out to sea. He doesn't deign to move aside as we pass. Then we turn our backs on the sea to go up to the de Roys'. The track winds between two lagoons, almost dry at this time of year. An ibis is asleep, with its head tucked under its wing. The cactus forest begins again above the lagoons, and we climb up some steps cut in the earth, then up a little stone stairway leading to a wooden bridge. From the bridge you can see right over the bay, which is blue now, streaked with a very pale orange. On the other side of the bridge is the de Roys' house. Some startled finches flutter up from the terrace.

It's nearly dawn. There's no time to lose. We leave the breakfast things and our two families set off. We go at a good pace, walking between the cacti and over basalt stones in precariously balanced layers, Laurence in the knapsack on my back. The stones shift as you tread on them, and if you stretch out your hands to save yourself, there are the cacti. We've brought water and a little food, but the de Roys don't usually take anything with them, even on an all-day trip. The basalt stones are very jagged and sharp, and cut through our rubber soles, tearing the canvas. You can easily wear out two pairs of tennis shoes in a day's hunting—which makes it an expensive sport in the Galápagos because everything comes from the mainland and it's difficult to earn money.

After walking for three-quarters of an hour we cross a rocky crevasse. Another hour and a half of cactus and we're beside the sea again, walking across jagged lava until we finally reach Turtle Bay. The beach is blindingly white, the sand so fine and powdery it clings to your skin like talc. We rest under the mango trees. Laurence crawls off and swallows handfuls of white powder, which doesn't appear to be indigestible: the sand is made of mother of pearl shells reduced to a fine powder by the sea. It's pure calcium.

By one of the headlands of the bay there are piles of marine iguanas one on top of another, warming themselves in the sun. They're big lizards—and are very gentle and easy to catch. Laurence can crawl faster than they can and catches them by their tails.

134

Their skin is very hard and their backs covered with great spikes like a dorsal crest. The first time you see their large mouths full of teeth you are very impressed. But André explained to us that when they are afraid they immobilize their adversaries by seizing them in their jaws but don't hurt them unless they try to pull away. A friend of his had to leave his wrist in a land iguana's mouth for twenty-four hours, and could only wait patiently until the animal was ready to release him. Marga's mother goes to sleep every night with three iguanas in her bed.

We walk—and walk. Tui, André's fourteen year old daughter, catches a kid but sets it free. Twice Christian sees some goats the others haven't noticed. He fires. André immediately carries out a surgeonlike dissection. He carefully opens up the animal and removes its entrails, taking care not to cut into the internal organs, as otherwise in this heat the meat would be spoiled at once. He delicately extracts the heart, liver, and kidneys. And the buzzards swoop down. They squat a few yards away and fix us with a terrible bright, piercing stare—waiting till we've gone. The flies are less ceremonious: they swarm in their thousands over the viscera with a muffled buzzing sound.

When the animal has been cleaned it's put in a gunny sack that one of the hunters carries over his shoulder. If it's too heavy to be carried in one piece it's cut up. The skin is removed with care, because Tui will scrape it and dry it to sell. Then the meat is cut into four joints. The innards are put in a little separate bag. The rest is left to the buzzards.

The billy goats are not shot unless they are very young, because they have too strong a flavor. One avoids killing the females that are feeding their young or in kid. Tui is only fourteen but she cuts up the animals as neatly as her father, and carries home a sixty- to eighty-pound goat on her shoulders like a man, running between the cactus plants and over stones for hours on end, without eating or drinking anything all day. Yet still she's slim and very feminine. Happiness at sea is also meeting people whose lives are different from other people's.

Finally, as Christian has shot four, we call a halt. We rest in some underground caves where the water is almost fresh, hardly brackish at all. We can quench our thirst and get cool—it's so hot

135

outside. On the way back, near Turtle Bay, we see some very tame wild ducks, stilt plovers, wild fowl, a wild ass. Wild—the word for this place, and a great part of our happiness.

We get back exhausted. Laurence is worn out after her long day and asleep in the rucksack. Jacqueline walks beside me to support her head. When we reach the de Roys' house at about six o'clock, the setting sun is turning the cacti violet, then purple. The sea shines like molten gold, and the silhouettes of the mangroves are as black as the lava and iguanas.

The gray heron in the lagoon is now a delicate pink. He takes a few dignified steps, his head held high.

Every morning, Christian goes to André's workshop to work on Gigi. It's a slow job because there is no electricity or welding equipment. Each flat iron bar has to be cut with a hack saw, then bored several times with a hand drill. It's important not to break the drill, which can't be replaced on Santa Cruz. The iron fittings are shaped with a vice, hammer, and tongs. The counterweight of the wind vane is lead melted in a jam can, which solidifies on the end of the iron rod supporting it. It's six days before Gigi II finally arrives aboard, painted white.

Once when I was washing clothes in sea water on the beach, I turned around to look for Laurence, who was crawling around— and she wasn't there. I instinctively looked in the water, all along the beach. No sign of her. I went toward a group of sea lions. Laurence was right in the middle of them. As soon as I approached, the old males moved menacingly toward me. What could I do? Call to Laurence? It might upset the males. So I did as she had done. I took off my bikini and knelt on all fours, then watched the sea lions' reaction. They hadn't budged. I advanced slowly, taking care not to lift my head so as not to frighten them, and managed to reach the herd and recover Laurence. We crawled away together on all fours, which Laurence thought was great fun.

The days pass, spent with the splendid de Roy family, who hunt for and classify shells and send them off to collectors and museums all over the world. In fifteen years they've shaped a life for themselves in this forgotten spot, a life of records and books, happy children and grownups.

136

Christian finishes the new tiller; the wood's so hard that when you're drilling you can't stop or the drill will stick. Tonight he's finished, and we take our poor old patched sails aboard. We're sad to be leaving the de Roys, who are a real family, as we hope to be, but we are happy at the thought of setting off again. How good it is to be poor and unencumbered, free to go where we like in our little *Alpha,* our small boat, with our baby, now ten months old. The boat is all we possess. If we lose her, we'll build another.

Yes, tonight it feels like a departure.

Where can we get fresh water?

"Go and see Forest Nelson," André tells us. "Tell him you have a baby on board and need a little water to cross the Pacific. He has quite a big supply. He won't say no."

Forest Nelson makes us a present of a ninety-gallon tankful, plus twenty-five gallons in a canvas water carrier. To get it aboard we have to get close to the village and shuttle between the boat and the shore with cans in André's boat. It takes us all morning.

As we want to take some fresh food and a few bags of rice, flour, etc., with us, we have to wait for the *Cristóbal Carrier,* which is due in soon. We can wait a few days. But how are we going to buy all we need for $3? We start swapping and bargaining. Christian sells a manila hawser, an old oilskin, and some nylon cord for $65, and Fritz buys the starter motor, dynamo, and battery, as Christian prefers starting the engine with the crank, which is more reliable. Fritz gives us a cast-iron frying pan, which I had always wanted. It was lying rusty in his loft and will be most useful. He exchanges a Primus with two burners, on gimbals, for our Camping Gaz. As his stove's an old one he also gives us $5. So we are now ready for the *Cristóbal Carrier.*

We buy our supplies by the sackload on the crowded deck. At this time of year oranges last only a few days, so I spend the rest of the day making marmalade. Alas, we haven't time to make lemonade. It's very easy to make: you put a little sugar in a bottle, pour on the juice, hermetically seal the bottle and keep it in a cool place where it won't get shaken up, i.e., on land, not on a boat. It will keep several years.

Didier has left on the *Klis* with Bernard. We're glad to be on our own for the long voyage ahead. Laurence makes less work now she's ten months old. She eats a little of everything, but I'm still feeding her as well. There's not much for a baby in the Galápagos. Jacqueline gives us some cans of Quaker oats, *petits-beurre* biscuits, eggs, milk—and some books. Christian gets our passports back from the harbor master's office and goes to Jimmy's to buy more supplies: he finds a box of vegetables, butter, a magnificent cheese, and a large bunch of bananas waiting there for us. And a letter from Mme. Horneman apologizing for not being able to offer us more, and wishing us *bon voyage.* We're very touched.

September 8, 1968. We set out. The de Roys are there at 7 A.M., with their boat full of presents. Several hot loaves come aboard, some goat fat, a beautiful cake made by Tui, who also gives us a goatskin and a little toy rabbit for Laurence, which she's been secretly making for the last few days.

We hoist the sails in glorious sunshine, with all the de Roy family on board. They go a mile with us, until we are beyond the bay, and then go back in their boat.

"The difference between you and us," Jacquelin says, "is that you're going, and we're staying."

"Au revoir."

"Write and tell us you're safe."

Laurence waves a chubby little hand. She probably thinks she'll be seeing Gil and Tui again shortly, as usual. But soon the boat is only a dark speck on the waves, while before us stretches the vast, empty Pacific, gleaming in the sunlight.

138

10

Apotheosis of the Pacific

Three thousand miles to go without seeing land or a boat. The *Alpha* cuts through the waves, leaving her white wake behind her, happy to have a month of clear sailing ahead. It's marvelous to be skimming along at five knots with the wind in our sails, while Gigi steers us and we do whatever we like in the cabin.

For a month we'll have only sea, sky, sun, and wind as our companions once more. Every day the sun will rise behind us, and set ahead of us, so we can check our compass by it. Happiness at sea. How miraculous it is, to be carried at will by our little water-tight steel boat to the other end of the world. In a month's time we'll be in the antipodes of France, having gone halfway round the world, and Laurence will be eleven months old. We will be in the middle of the largest ocean in the world—and at home.

I'm tired and doze on my bunk. Laurence, little early riser that she is, comes to have her feed. My eyes are shut and she doesn't dare wake me. But she's hungry. She comes so close I can feel her breath. Then she taps me softly. When I open my eyes she smiles broadly and climbs on the bunk. Afterward she waits for me to get dressed and go ashore. She can't understand why we're still in bed when the sun's shining.

Sail on, *Alpha,* toward the west. Last night the wind increased. At daybreak we lost sight of Fernandina, the last island. There'll be no more land until the Marquesas Islands, and no merchant shipping lanes. Our only chart of the Pacific Ocean is the pilot index chart for June, July, and August, which a cargo ship in Panama gave us; it is not very detailed. The Marquesas are indicated by small dots. But we've managed to do Panama-Cocos-Galápagos with it, so we ought to be able to get as far as the Marquesas Islands.

Christian leaps to resecure Gigi, who is leaning overboard. I put Laurence in the cabin and take the tiller. With this strong wind behind us I'm uneasy. One of the pins of the plate that anchors Gigi to the boat has sunk to the bottom of the Pacific. Christian looks for another in the galley drawer, which is overflowing with nuts, bolts, screws, nails, small fittings—taken from old bits of wood, from attics, or just picked up in the street. In three months' time, true to family tradition, Laurence would be able to pick up all the nails and bits of iron that she found on the quay in Papeete, putting them carefully in her little bucket—"for my Daddy."

Christian finally has to get into the icy water to fix Gigi's plate with a new bolt.

Still the same perfect weather every day when we wake up, the same regular existence following the sun. Christian lies on his bunk for hours on end, reading. He glances at the compass by his side from time to time, at the mainsail overhead, and at Gigi: there's no need to get up. We talk more and more about our next boat—or, if worst comes to worst, the changes we'll make on this one.

The de Roys had a marvelous idea—they gave Laurence a pile of old newspapers to tear up and make into confetti and to roll into balls. She's already been at it for three days and has just learned something very important: you must never throw anything in the water. She was playing in the cockpit, picked up a bit of crumpled

140

paper, and threw it overboard. What a wonderful game. You throw it and watch where it drops, and with a bit of luck it will float and bob over the waves before disappearing. I had to smack her hand to show her she mustn't do that. Otherwise, Daddy's tools, Mummy's crockery, clothes—and anything else—would all end up in the sea. She has never thrown anything else overboard and quickly understood that everything that falls in the water is lost for good.

Sunday, September 15. Our seventh day at sea. We've done 900 miles, which makes 128 miles a day. It's still fine, but the wind is stronger and is on the quarter. We're being buffeted about and the boat is often swamped by a huge wave that hits us broadside, making us heel over. Laurence turns her back to the waves in the cockpit. But each time a large one arrives, she crouches down and holds on as tightly as she can, as if knowing she could be washed overboard. Except that I'm always close beside her, of course.

Last night, one of these wretched waves crashed through the open hatch into the cabin and drenched Christian, inundating the quarter berth. This morning I must dry the lemons, onions, and cassava. I can't walk around bare-topped any more. Laurence has grown so much that as soon as she sees my bare breasts she rushes up with her best smile and insists on having a feed, for the sheer pleasure of it. I'd like to wean her completely, but it's out of the question before we get to the Polynesian Islands, because it's an extra safeguard. Last night I broke the Thermos and this morning our poor little girl had a stray splinter of glass in her mouth.

One day follows another, uninterruptedly. This pleasant monotony gives Christian and me a chance to rediscover one another —our dream is coming true at last: we are alone on our boat with our little daughter, who is getting bigger every day. We are happy.

During these long peaceful moments we look back over the past few years to our meeting in Papeete—it has all gone so fast. We haven't had time to take it in. Three years have passed in a rush; we hadn't really begun to grasp that we were two people, now three, whose destinies are linked forever. It's only now we are stunned at this realization, as if it had all happened in a dream. We love our happiness at sea; our little daughter who makes it come true for us. We don't feel like a married couple, but like lovers who meet now and then and steal a little space of time from life.

This crossing is the last one on the way to Tahiti; our lodestar, our starting and end point, the island to which we always return. Tahiti. The only port we love between America and Japan. Only nine hours by plane from Los Angeles—a month the way we travel. It sometimes makes you wonder why we chose this life.

The wind is much stronger, at least force seven, and the *Alpha* is going at a terrific pace. From time to time the jib collapses for a few seconds and then suddenly fills again with a tremendous crack. Gigi is shaking badly. How long will she hold?

But this morning the sun is shining as usual, and Laurence is kicking in her bath. Our noon position shows that we have gone 270 miles in 48 hours. A little too far south perhaps, but what a pace! We sing with joy. Christian plays the guitar and Laurence dances.

Crrrraaack! I'm the one who catches Gigi this time. The fitting that holds her to the deck has broken. As it was welded we have to think a moment how to replace it. I hold on as best I can to Gigi, and Christian secures her to the stern pulpit with a bit of metal rod. But the wind increases in strength and two hours later the rod breaks.

I take up my position on guard again, and at the same moment the mainsail gets a six-foot tear. Then Christian gets a bit of stainless-steel wire left over from the rigging and fixes Gigi, who has never worked better. She doesn't rock or shake at all, and is beautifully supple.

Now to work. We lower the mainsail, removing it completely. We mend the sail until midnight, drunk with fatigue, and finally hoist it.

And the days pass, bringing a dead calm. You have to be able to take anything on a long crossing, and to have nerves of iron. Day after day we continue our slow and painful progress, unable to do anything except wait for the wind to come up.

We have to be on watch all the time, without a break—no Sundays off. A crossing means a month's ceaseless struggle to reach your goal.

Laurence has sunstroke, a temperature of 100 degrees. Laurence's fever makes us take the calms and light airs as bad auguries. We both, silently, remember possible dangers: the baby falling overboard, inadequate suit of sails, danger of appendicitis, and so on. But neither of us says anything and we keep up an appearance of calm optimism in front of Laurence.

Note in the skipper's log:

> *A small boat is sailing through the night at a few miles an hour, leaving behind her a long phosphorescent wake under the starry sky. It's very dark and there's no one to see this little speck of light bobbing over the waves. In this moving "capsule" lives a little family, who hope and fear, and sing, 1,500 miles from the nearest land. Thousands of miles of sea to cross, alone, in a "tin can" propelled by a few square yards of sail rotted by a year's sun, sea, rain, wind. But today I feel unusually relaxed. We'll be in Tahiti in a few weeks' time. We'll be able to swim for hours in the warm sea, lie on a white sandy beach surrounded by trees and flowers.*

Laurence is always disappearing now. Yesterday I managed to grab her just as she was calmly climbing over the rail. I didn't scream, but last night, at about two in the morning, she woke up sobbing as if she'd just had a nightmare and went to cuddle up against Christian, much to his surprise.

The fishing is no better than the wind: the Pacific is as disappointing as the Atlantic was generous. It isn't that there aren't any fish, but there are probably too many big ones that snatch our catch before we've had a chance to draw it in. We've already lost two spoons. As often as not there's only a bit of the head of our fish left on the hook, after it's been stolen by a larger one.

"I really think I've learned more in this year at sea than during my whole youth," notes Christian. *"This life enriches one, even if there are moments of emptiness and pointlessness."*

Meeting the de Roys gave us a lot to think about. If we decide to go back to civilization and live ashore, who will bring up our children? School, television, posters, youth groups, evening classes, pediatricians, and, in ever-increasing numbers, psychologists. When will we see them? In the evening when they come home to wash, eat, and go to bed; in the morning when they're getting ready for school. Which leaves Sundays. But it's difficult to carry on a conversation from one Sunday to the next with one's children, especially when parents and children are not sharing the same life. Home becomes almost like a hotel for grownups and children, with the mother in most cases being reduced to everyone's servant. What it really means is that the father and mother work for children whom they don't have the pleasure of bringing up, whom they don't have the pleasure of seeing enjoy the best part of the day—and the children become more and more deprived. Parents and children no longer have any work in common.

We don't believe this is what family life is about.

On land, however, it's very difficult to escape the system. The only solution is the one the de Roys have tried—find a desert island. Even that isn't a complete solution because children need to rub up against each other, get to know the advantages and pitfalls of society, so that they can choose the kind of life they want. It's up to us to give them the chance to live happily in whatever way they choose.

Living on a yacht enables one to combine various possibilities. We can live and work in a large town for a year without leaving the boat, and then live in a village for a year. There are excellent school correspondence courses. I've discovered a marvelous one that is very modern and adaptable, as its name implies: *Pédagogie Moderne.* And there's nothing to stop one from sending the children to school for a few months from time to time, to learn a foreign language or come into more direct competition with others.

An enormous whale—larger than the boat—surfaces only a few yards from the *Alpha.* We keep absolutely quiet so as not to frighten it. The monster dives down right beside us several times, going under the *Alpha*'s keel and reappearing on the other side. If it judges the distance incorrectly it will give us a very nasty jolt. But luckily it doesn't touch us—and hasn't come to scratch its back on the hull like the sharks. It keeps us company until the sun goes down, and disappears when it grows dark.

The *Alpha* advances about one hundred miles every day, in spite of so little wind. It's marvelous to know we're making progress, that each day we're one hundred miles nearer the Marquesas Islands, where we will find some childhood friends. And now there's a crescent moon to complete this happy day. How brightly it shines in the clear sky! It's warm and we stay on deck for a while.

Tonight at sunset, Laurence begins to sigh with tiredness, while still continuing to climb, bathe, play, and jump around. She

144

has only one rest during the day, which doesn't go on very long however quiet we are so as not to disturb her. She loves sleeping on the ground, on the clean, hard floor, without mattress or bed-clothes. In port, she likes lying on the iron of the deck.

But today she's overdone it. Christian takes her in his arms in the cockpit and she snuggles down while I get the dinner. It's my "What are we going to eat tonight?" time. Refreshed, Laurence sits up at the table with us to share our meal.

Afterward the toys have to be cleared away, and the paper confetti, and I sing to her to send her off to sleep. Then there's the blissful peace of evening.

Apart from our mail, which we won't get until we get to Papeete, I'm in no hurry to arrive. I feel I am on holiday for the first time in my life. My household tasks seem easy, almost nonexist-ent. I read and continue my studies of English and graphology most of the day. I can enjoy watching Laurence's progress, how she's trying to say new words. "No" is easy. How wonderful for a child to discover a new means of communicating with others: your first smile, the first syllables you discover when you learn to read, your first love—the wonder can last a lifetime.

> *What a difference between sailing here and in the Mediterranean* (it says in the ship's log). *Here our oilskins are rotting in the forecastle, under a bag of shoes in which I've also hidden the bottles of Côtes de Provence I brought from the Mas du Mournaï so that they could go round the world. I regret the time about three weeks ago, when it was still cool enough to wear a sweater because of the Humboldt Current. But I have no regrets for the Mediterranean at all, probably because my boat's no longer new and I'd like to refit it throughout. It feels marvelous to be sailing toward Tahiti, master of one's own boat. Naked, tanned, and in great form! In a year's sailing, calling in at ports, we have moved nine hours westward, an hour every 600 miles.*

We can't hear Radio Tahiti yet, but it shouldn't be long, be-cause there's a relay station in the Marquesas Islands. It's good that the moon is waxing; we will arrive by moonlight as we did in Barbados.

It smells like arriving, like land.

While we write a few letters, Laurence jumps about, sings, and does all sorts of dangerous climbs. She's impossible, as always when we're getting close to land. There it is. Christian has Radio Tahiti —we're there. It feels like home when we hear the familiar voices. We leave the radio on for the pleasure of hearing French and Tahitian spoken and sung. But we have to keep our eyes open for any land ahead. At about nine-thirty the moon shines so brightly you could read a newspaper.

Christian goes on deck every half hour. Suddenly at about 3 A.M.: "France, come and look." A black shape is visible on the great barren expanse of the ocean, where there has been nothing for twenty-six days: it's Ua Huka. Our throats feel tight and we can't speak. We are both thinking the same thing, and a phrase goes round and round in our heads, dizzily repeated like a crazy jingle on a poster: We are in Polynesia. It is the *Alpha*'s moment of triumph, the moment when the film music crescendos at the close of a story that might have ended sadly but is triumphant.

What a night! We don't want to slow down because we want to get to Nuku Hiva quickly. The two most important centers in the Marquesas Islands are Atuona and Taiohae. We have friends at Taiohae who will certainly have news of the *Klis,* of Didier. We'll go there.

Christian continues going on deck every half hour throughout the night, but we don't sight land again until 6 A.M. When the sun rises, we're not dreaming. Nuku Hiva is there before us. A long way off, on the port side, we can just make out Ua Pu, the island with mountain peaks that look like the fingers of a hand. There are no reefs in the Marquesas; the islands rise sheer from deep water as in the Galápagos. Luckily the wind is just strong enough to allow us time to identify each bay and cape. We pass the deep inlet at Taipi or the Baie du Contrôleur, and at 2 P.M. enter Taiohae, skimming past one of the Guardians—the two black rocks that stand one on each side of the entrance to the bay, like giant statues.

The anchor is dropped at last on the black sandy bottom, and we furl our sails. We are in the Marquesas. They give us a warm welcome at the *gendarmerie,* because they were anxiously awaiting our arrival: our friend Jacques, in Paris, horrified that our family had had no news of us for over four months, had asked the French navy to search for us. Luckily the navy doesn't panic; they are used

146

to the ways of yachtsmen. They waited a bit and Didier, arriving on the *Klis,* told them we were in the Galápagos. But Didier had been gone nearly a month, and the *gendarmerie* were anxious to see us arrive.

The Marquesas Islands are typically French Polynesia, with all its softness, limpid beauty, and natural delicacy. There is time to live—to breathe. In Italy, or Spain, or Morocco, or the Galápagos, you hardly ever see girls or young women in the village streets, but here you see them everywhere—lightly dressed in gay *pareos,* with pretty flowers in their beautiful dark hair and smiling, open faces. They are proud but not arrogant, with a natural grace. With them are well-built young men who are just as beautiful.

Everyone seems to be calm, serene; they smile in a relaxed, friendly way, with no trace of nervousness, or fear or complexes. The only thing that matters is to live, without complicating life unnecessarily. Hunting, fishing, keeping one's house clean, sculpting, working are things which one does unhurriedly, without continually watching the clock, without continually complaining how hard life is. Life is no less hard than in other countries, but here one always looks on the bright side. Even the color for mourning is white.

In Europe, if two bicyclists crash into each other there is a torrent of abuse. Here, they sit on the ground for a minute, and laugh loudly. It is said that morals are loose here: this middle-class stricture, full of insinuation that may or may not be true, describes rather an attitude to life. The family is very much alive in Polynesia, and it is sacred. It is put before everything else. In Polynesia there are no orphanages or centers for homeless children or unmarried mothers. There is always a grandmother, an aunt, or a friend who will welcome a baby with open arms.

Children are not "coddled." They are treated with affection but as people in their own right. You see little fishermen of three, as dignified as their fathers. Polynesians don't chuck them under the chin, or make "sacrifices" for them. They simply aim in the most natural way in the world to let children and adults live as happy and balanced lives as possible. One finds this philosophy of happiness in all the islands of the three archipelagos: the Marquesas, Tuamotu, and Society Islands.

We are beginning our stay in the Marquesas with a month's holiday with childhood friends. Josée, a blue-eyed Bretonne, was at school with my sister. She is head of the kindergarten at the Catholic Mission School, to which her parents devoted their lives, and has three adorable children. Her husband, Laurent Haïti, a tall, good-looking Marquesian, is a sculptor. He aims to revive lost art forms. When the first Protestant missionaries reached these islands, they destroyed everything of a religious—and therefore artistic—nature they could lay their hands on. It took years of research to find any trace of the lost works. This is why you sometimes find wooden or stone *tikis* buried in the ground, which have survived only because they were hidden. But the missionaries couldn't destroy the great stone *tikis* six feet high, or the chiefs' tombs, cut in the rock above seventy-five-foot-high precipices, which you can see in the valley where Laurent's family lives, at Hakaui.

Christian is building a dinghy for us, with Laurent, and fishes for crayfish at night in the river, and goes goat hunting. Laurence takes her first steps, and has her first birthday—we blow out one candle on the boat. The time passes so quickly; already a month's gone and my sister wrote to me a year ago saying she was going to fly from Tahiti to Paris on October 31. I would like to see her if only for an hour. So on Sunday, October 20, we set sail for the Tuamotu Archipelago and Tahiti.

We have a week's tricky sailing to begin with. Luckily we're fit and rested after our month in the Marquesas Islands. Tahiti is giving us the cold shoulder. This blasted adverse wind. I begin to feel more and more I won't see my sister before October 31. When will I see her again? If she travels as much as I do it will be several years before we meet.

On the 27th, it says in capital letters in the log book: DRIFTING WRECK SAILS IN TATTERS. What a night. This morning the boat is in chaos and we look ghastly. The wind, still in our teeth, got much stronger last night and it was so dark you couldn't see more than sixty feet ahead. And the fear of the atolls all round us, kept us awake in spite of all our recent sleepless nights. We took turns on watch all night, but in fact we were both constantly awake, our ears pricked, our eyes straining in vain to see through the darkness. The angry waves submerged the boat and then lifted us up to amazing heights.

Toward midnight, when Christian had been on watch for four hours, a tear several yards long appeared in the jib. It took him an hour, lying flat on his front and ceaselessly inundated by the waves, to lower it and put up in its place the storm jib.

The atolls are probably quite near; there may be some right in front of us. But it's impossible to see breakers or hear them thundering on a reef because the wind and sea are making too much noise. If we see one, at the last minute, it will probably be too late to do anything. We are strained and tense, not knowing where the sea may hit us next. Luckily a watch like that keeps all your senses alert and leaves no time for fear or reflection.

The mainsail is flapping horribly. At about 5 A.M. Christian decides to take in another reef. While he's winding the reefing handle of the revolving boom, and with difficulty preventing himself from falling, a six-foot tear appears in the sail. We lower it and replace it with the white storm jib. The sea is still raging and keeps washing over us. There's no question of stopping at the Tuamotu Islands. At dawn, the sun comes up, but the sea is still angry.

Our noon position places us to the south of the last two Tuamotu Islands, Matahiva and Tikehau. We must have passed between the two atolls last night, when the storm was at its height —without knowing or seeing anything.

We are safe and sound. The only annoying thing is that the wind is still against us and we only have thirty square feet of sail to play with. We're unlikely to arrive in Tahiti before October 31. How many days will it take us with our reduced canvas? When the wind's strong, we make some headway, but as soon as it drops, it feels as though we're going backward. Christian is talking seriously about rationing our food and water, because we could drift for a month or two before we reach land.

At worst, we'll hit Bora Bora, but we won't miss the islands. Miserably tossed to and fro, we are making some progress. We must be because Moorea is there, seven miles ahead of us. How good it is to reach this familiar island. I feel we've arrived already, that I can smell Papeete in my nostrils.

Moorea is there, but the wind drops more and more, preventing us from reaching land. We hoist our patched sails again, hoping there's life in them yet. We skim along for an hour, and begin to hope we'll be there in a few hours. But after an hour the mainsail tears across. We reef it. It tears again. Christian starts the engine. We're making no headway. There's probably a rope round the propeller. We both have sore throats and are not at all anxious to get into the water. It's maddening to be becalmed, or as good as becalmed, so near our goal. The worst of it is that it could go on like this for several days, just long enough to miss my sister.

Laurence can do more and more on her own, finding herself bananas and biscuits and lying down fully dressed, as we do, when she's tired.

In spite of his sore throat and a temperature of 102 degrees, Christian dives in at 4 A.M. to clear the propeller. Then, as he can't sleep, he goes on with the repairs, dismantling the fuel filter, which is encrusted with dirty fuel from the Galápagos, which we had in fact filtered once. Then he starts the engine. There's just enough juice to get us to Tahiti.

At daybreak we're on a level with Moorea at last. Christian sleeps for an hour and I take the tiller as Tahiti approaches.

At last, at 9 A.M., we drop anchor in Papeete harbor, alongside Paul Smet's *Tiare.*

We are in Tahiti. Now we're here, our exhaustion seems less. I rush to find my sister, who hugs Laurence delightedly and says she's not going to France after all.

We are in Tahiti—October, 1968.

Pierre and Catherine Deshumeur, who saw us arrive from the *Vencia,* come aboard: "Mmm, it smells good on your boat. You can tell you've just arrived." Other yachts appear, or leave, and we make new friends every day. Christian does tourist trips on the *Alpha* with her tattered sails.

Laurence has found a friend: Elodie, a fair-haired three-year-old on the *Ophélie.* When the two little girls both try at the same time to go along the plank leading from one boat to the other, they sometimes tumble in the water.

Also here is Julio Villar, the only Spanish solo navigator, who

150

speaks French perfectly. He has sailed around the world, but his dinghy is so small it will take only one person. If you move at all you're liable to capsize: he made it from half a sheet of plywood. Papeete harbor is full of every kind of boat from April to September, especially large American racing yachts, which are sailing round the world and call in at Tahiti before setting out for the Indian Ocean.

Then there's Bernard Moitessier, who, like us, will be here for some time. We all congregate every evening on the few blades of grass that Bernard Moitessier proudly calls our lawn and that we carefully water so that it will last as long as possible, or until the quay is rebuilt. We share some raw fish *à la Tahitienne,* salad, and fruit, and chat—exchanging memories: a desert island, a forgotten or lost beach, a dangerous reef, a recipe for preserving food. We talk of Cape Horn, Patagonia, the Galápagos, or the Indian Ocean, as people in Paris talk of their country houses. We try to learn all we can about the Torres Strait, Indonesia, the Chagos archipelago, so that we will be able to avoid the worst dangers. And we dream. The little girls watch and listen, and ask their first questions.

And now, a new boat is taking shape, the fruit of all our experience, our dreams. We sell the *Alpha* in Tahiti and move back to France, to Equiheen to count our money. We must go to Marquentaire to see M. Knocker, the designer of Bernard's *Joshua;* that's the sort of boat we want.

On November 5, 1970, our new boat, her hull bare, rusty, with no deck, nothing but a Yanmar diesel engine, is brought down the Rhône through the freezing weather and horrible fogs.

151

11

Pygmalion

Now begins the terrible winter of the great building operation. The Lyon-Marseille motorway is blocked by snow, and four thousand stranded motorists await Christmas among the freezing snow banks. Christian is building the *Pygmalion* single-handed, in Marseille, in the constant biting wind. He sleeps and eats on board. Although he's hardly ever wielded a hammer and saw, he's doing it all himself. It's a miracle he isn't ill. On the coldest night of the winter it's twenty degrees in the boat, in spite of having two heaters on all day.

At last, in May, the *Pygmalion* is launched. I've been signing people up for sailing lessons. We hope to make our living that way this summer. The *Pygmalion* is not luxurious but is an excellent boat. In June, she sets out for Greece, and returns via Malta, Tunisia,

Sardinia, Corsica. We have numerous "crew" for our sailing school.

As winter nears, the Mediterranean becomes more and more chancy. We are leaving Marseille for the sun of the Tropics. One has to be prepared for frequent squalls at this time of year, and Christian and I both are secretly apprehensive, as if we somehow felt we shouldn't tempt the devil, as if a voice were telling us we should be satisfied with our first voyage from France to Tahiti with our baby. I dread this crossing as far as Gibraltar, and am glad Roger and Jean-Baptiste are with us: they are excellent divers and fish in the Mediterranean even in the middle of winter. They've never done any sailing, but they're big, strong men and very cooperative.

Laurence is now four. Although she's always been used to sailing, she's still very young and has to be looked after all the time.

Monday, November 8. I look at my galley with its rows of lovely new labeled tins: flour, sugar, rice, pasta. Our *Pygmalion* is all new and shining, freshly painted and in perfect shape. A whole vanload of supplies have disappeared into the lockers. And at eleven-thirty we're off—under the engine as there really isn't enough wind for the sails, which seem to hesitate in the light breeze. A yacht and a launch accompany us, with some of our friends. The sun is very hot and we put on our bathing things and Laurence wears a grass skirt. We're all busy framing each other in our camera lenses and using up a lot of film. Addresses are hurriedly exchanged in the frenzy of departure and visitors' books signed. By one o'clock we're alone at last, that is Christian, Laurence, and I, with Roger and Jean-Baptiste.

Our first lunch at sea. In our bathing things on deck, in November. Marvelous. I'm wallowing in luxury: I have rubber gloves for dishwashing, and hot running water. I think of all the good things I'm going to cook in the days to come. I'm beginning to feel blasé. Now that I have a good Primus on gimbals, I only need a steady stomach to see me through.

At 8 P.M. France-Inter forecasts wind veering to the southwest in the Mediterranean, which wouldn't really suit us as we're making for the Balearics. But for the moment there's no wind from the southwest. A light northeasterly breeze gets up as it gets dark, while we're having the second, and last, meal of our four-day voyage—only we didn't know that then.

Christian is on watch until midnight: the wind's gradually increasing. I watch the speedometer from my bunk. We're carrying our usual area of sail, that is, three hundred square feet. At midnight Jean-Baptiste takes his turn. The wind's still increasing and a swell is beginning. It must be the mistral. Christian goes on deck and decides to bear away from the wind. We keep all the sails set. The tiller is increasingly hard to handle—we haven't a wheel. During the whole of Jean-Baptiste's watch the wind continues to increase and the seas to build up.

Christian notes:

At 3 A.M. I lower the mainsail. My two fellow crewmates for the week have never been on a boat before and can only stand and watch. 120 square feet is quite a handful in this gale. And in the pitch dark you have to be careful the halyard doesn't catch halfway down the mast, because there's nothing worse than a sail half down and flapping itself to pieces. Shouting to the helmsman to keep downwind, I begin my perilous climb, hand over hand up the mast, with the help of the halyards and shrouds. By an incredible effort I reach the jammed rope. I try desperately to free it, but it won't budge and I have to shout to Jean-Baptiste to bring me the knife I'd left in my oilskin. While he's looking for it I manage to heave myself up another three yards and free the halyard with my toe. And all this while the boat rocks to and fro with me hanging by my arms to the smooth, slippery mast. I slither down to the deck thirty feet below, trembling from my exertions, and tackle the difficult job of furling the sail.

4 A.M., Tuesday, November 9. Roger takes his turn on deck. He has more and more difficulty controlling the tiller. Christian goes up and decides to lower the jib: *"The jib isn't much easier. No net under the bowsprit jutting over the sea, and sometimes completely submerged in the waves. I cling on so as not to be torn off by the water and manage to take advantage of a brief respite to furl the sail and lash it securely."*

Christian takes down the mizzen as well. By morning there's only the storm jib, which is suffering badly. The wind's still rising and we're flying along, at eight or ten knots, and the speedometer, which doesn't go beyond ten knots, keeps sticking. We must easily be doing twelve knots with just the storm jib. At about 8 A.M., Jean-Baptiste and Christian lower the storm jib. We're running at least six knots under bare poles, and at times at ten knots or more.

The patent log is squeaking horribly. The swell is still building up, with white crests. The waves are short, very steep, with troughs of almost thirty feet. We are beginning to roll in all directions. Roger, on deck, exhausted, has been submerged several times. He's only prevented himself from being dragged overboard by holding on to the tiller, with great difficulty. We're all wearing harnesses and go on deck as little as possible.

Seasickness strikes below. We each have a little blue bucket. Even Laurence is sick several times, but she's very brave and doesn't cry or complain. I'm sick too, for the third time since I was seven. The waves continually wash over the deck and the water is beginning to come in more and more. We have to shut the hatch. The water is icy, the air's freezing cold, and the helmsman is drenched through in spite of his oilskin, with his fingers red and swollen with cold, and the salt water stinging his eyes.

When I read Bernard Moitessier's *The Long Way,* I was horrified to learn that the *Joshua* did six to ten knots under bare poles. I thought this kind of thing only happened in high latitudes. I would never have imagined the same thing could happen to us in the Gulf of Lions. The wind and sea are making such a din you can't hear yourself speak outside. You have to yell. The helmsman has to use immense concentration to see he's not taken unawares, and to keep the *Pygmalion* heading into the waves. This is made more difficult because they are very choppy, and coming from all directions, as if the wind were veering from port to starboard all the time.

10:30. Next watch. Jean-Baptiste takes the tiller. Roger comes below and crawls shivering into his sleeping bag on the floor by my bunk. Christian, in the same state, is stretched out against the galley partition. We are all on the side the boat's listing, except Laurence, who's asleep on the bunk opposite mine. The breakers must be thirty feet high now. They crash down on the helmsman, on the stern, and on the starboard bow, thundering down on the deck with a great roar.

Craaack!

Christian leaps on deck. The mizzen boom has broken in two. A wave smacked it violently into the shrouds. Jean-Baptiste just had time to duck down or his skull would have been fractured. The sky is pitch dark and the white raging sea is running in all directions.

We're reaching the end of our strength [*Christian wrote*]. *With incredible effort I manage to drop the sea anchor over the bow, at the end of a good strong rope of 22-mm. nylon. The pull is terrific, but the boat refuses to head into the wind and waves. And it is hit so savagely on the beam that I have to cut the rope quickly, fearing the worst. Seeing that it would soon be impossible for anyone to hold the tiller, I make a sea anchor with some canvas to drag from the stern—again with the hope of getting the boat headed into the waves. No good. I haven't the strength to set the storm jib, or to send a message on my automatic transmitter. I'm afraid my safety harness will break, and have to keep throwing myself at the mast when a great wall of water sweeps over us. I go on deck several times, although I'm exhausted, to lower the sails one by one as the wind rises. Finally I attach any ropes I can find, with weights on the ends, as drag lines, to try to slow down the boat.*

At about 1 P.M. Jean-Baptiste sees a monstrous wave approaching from off the quarter, much larger than the others and piling up with an ear-splitting roar. He pushes the tiller over as hard as he can, but he's already completely submerged. Both the *Pygmalion's* masts are under water and her keel's in the air. Jean-Baptiste tries desperately not to breathe and the seconds drag as he waits for the boat to right herself. Then he clings to the starboard stay, on the side away from the list, thinking he won't be submerged there, not realizing that the boat's done a complete somersault. But immediately a second gigantic wave breaks over her, driving both masts under and lifting the keel in the air, smacking the boat into the water and crashing down on the keel with incredible force again and again. Jean-Baptiste takes the tiller at once and rights the boat, stern to the waves. "A moment later," he recalled:

"I found myself at the bottom of the sea before I knew what was happening. I had to tell myself to keep calm. I said: 'You're at the bottom of the sea; you'd better not get drowned.' Luckily my harness held, or I would definitely have had it. It's a great keel, but

156

when you see it like that it looks pretty strange. It gave me a terrible fright. My legs were like jelly. I stayed on deck for seven hours in that weather, thinking, 'They're all right down there; it's better if they don't see this.' "

Meanwhile below cans are bursting out of the lockers and raining down on us. The wind's howling and I keep thinking the forehatch will be washed away. Then what will we do? Before we can put it back we'll have shipped a good bit of water, and a steel boat sinks rapidly when it's full of water. Lost in my worries, I'm taken by surprise and suddenly find myself in complete darkness, pinioned under a heavy mass of planks, with splinters of glass all over my face. I can't see anything, or breathe. I push frantically to try to free myself—but it's no use. I realize we've turned completely over, with the masts in the water. I have time to think that if the ballast comes away we've had it. Even if it were possible to get out of the boat in a sea like this—which is most improbable—it would be quite impossible to reach the life raft. And we wouldn't last long in the icy water, with those waves.

I can see only one thing: Laurence's face.

I gradually see a crack of light appearing—we're righting ourselves. Where is my daughter? I can't hear anyone and the planks pressing on me are stopping my breathing. I shout: "I'm suffocating! Quick! Where's Laurence?"

"She's all right," Roger shouts. "I'm coming."

He has to move several planks and then leans against the hull and pushes as hard as he can. My bunk has overturned and I'm covered with cans. But I'm unhurt except for some cuts on my hands and a splinter of glass eight millimeters long in my right eye. It's agonizing, and doesn't come out until twenty-four hours later.

Roger had seen all the floor planks, the carpet, metal fittings, tools, cans of paint, oil, varnish, etc., come tumbling down on our bunks. Laurence was catapulted over it all in her bunk, which did a revolution of 180 degrees, meaning she must have made an incredibly dangerous flight through the air. A hundred pounds of cans and goodness knows how many ropes had fallen with her on top of me. Some jars crashed on the ceiling, which had dents made by the jars and a small split. The eggs broke on the portholes.

Christian is upright, with his left leg caught under my bunk.

157

Roger and I heave with all our might to free him. Then there's a brief respite. Roger holds Laurence in his arms amid the planks, trying to reassure her and keep her warm. We can't put anything back until we reach land. We each sit in the corner we've chosen, surrounded by debris. Christian is the first to remember that Jean-Baptiste is still on deck. We realize with shame that we hadn't even given him a thought. I burst into tears.

All the starboard lockers have burst open and come adrift. The air cylinder has torn away the table leg to which it was fixed and has been hurled into the galley, where there is complete chaos. It is stripped of everything, including the two-burner Primus, which is hidden under a mountain of cans, broken eggs, chocolate.

In the main saloon there is an awful smell from the pots of paint, and toxic fumes. In the forecastle a full cylinder of gas has broken loose with a snapped pipe and the gas was escaping for at least half an hour before we noticed anything. What can we do? We can't keep the forehatch open because the water's flooding in, although it might be safer. We can't possibly light a match down here. Roger insists on staying in the saloon, saying there's very little gas.

I'm perched on the companion ladder with Laurence, with jets of water hitting me full in the face. I try going down but immediately feel as if my head's in a vice. I tell Roger to come out—he's beginning to feel dizzy. We leave the hatchway open. In the cockpit, Jean-Baptiste smells a strong odor of escaping gas from below. The conditions are so bad outside we have to urinate in the hold.

"Shut the hatch," Jean-Baptiste yells. But Christian decides drowning is better than being gassed. Laurence is completely submerged for a minute, inundated on the rear berth; she's drenched right through. She stays wet like that all night, sleeping beside me in an equally sodden blanket. But she doesn't complain, even though she hasn't eaten in over twenty-four hours.

The automatic pilot has disappeared. Our life raft has slipped three yards. The dinghy over it is held against the cabin top by the boom, and luckily is tightly wedged. The skipper makes sure with a strong bit of line. You never know in weather like this. No one has mentioned being shipwrecked, but such things do happen, even to the best people. And if it gets worse, with the sea like this it

158

would be impossible to get aboard any boat that came to our rescue. If we had to use our life raft, could we even launch it? How it roars!

Jean-Baptiste, Christian, Laurence, and I are all huddled in what remains of the rear-berth. The hatch is open and we're getting drenched. Laurence is not asleep but pressing up against me to keep warm. I'll hold her until we get to Barcelona, because she's had a nasty fright. And she's so wet it's the only way to keep her warm.

By some miracle, in the midst of all this chaos, her toys and clothes are safe. Ironically, although some fine books on navigation are trailing in the paint, the crockery is broken, and all the contents of the refrigerator and the fresh food are inedible, a few ridiculous things like my rubber gloves are still hanging, untouched, as if nothing had happened.

Roger is at the helm. The tiller bar is beginning to bend, and it becomes more and more difficult to steer. At about 9 P.M. Christian relieves Roger. The breakers are a little less high. The wind doesn't seem to have eased off at all but the swell has diminished: we are just leaving the middle of the Gulf of Lions. Christian suddenly appears below with the bar of the tiller in his hand.

"The tiller's broken. There are only a couple of inches left. There's nothing I can do. We'll try to mend it tomorrow morning. We'll just have to drift tonight." A steel tiller broken, but the boat's sound, which is the main thing.

All five of us are on the rear berth. We keep getting tangled up. One or another of us keeps getting up to see if there isn't a boat on the horizon that might come to our rescue. I tell myself that any boat would be in exactly the same state. Still, the essential parts of *Pygmalion* are sound: masts, rigging, hull, portholes are all absolutely intact. Our only major mistake was the gas cylinder, which we intended to keep on deck during the voyage. But you can't afford to make mistakes at sea, even for a second. We're doing at least five knots, still under bare poles, with no one at the helm. And the *Pygmalion* is keeping a disconcertingly steady course to the west.

Wednesday, November 10. Roger finds a hacksaw among the debris and tries to cut off the smashed end of the tiller bar to make it usable. He works very carefully so as not to break the blade: we'd never find another in this mess. The stump of the tiller has swollen, so Roger pushes the bar into the metal just above the stump and

159

drives it in with a hammer. He reinforces it with a metal bar, bound with strong rope.

Christian and Jean-Baptiste hoist the sails as the wind drops more and more, preventing us from reaching land, which is still in sight by nightfall. As there is no sun or stars, and no visibility, we have no idea where we are. We only know we're heading toward the north of Spain.

During the day Jean-Baptiste and Christian bail out the bilges as best they can. The quick-drying paint has completely blocked up our pump, and only a pathetic trickle of water comes out. Actually, we haven't shipped much water, which proves to us the advantages of having only two small openings in the deck—the forehatch, which is always shut at sea, and the companion hatch, which is only two feet across.

During the night of Wednesday-Thursday we see a light ahead, slightly to starboard. Is it Barcelona or the Balearic Islands? At about 4 A.M. we identify the Barcelona light.

On Thursday morning, we sail into the harbor, under canvas. The engine compartment is full of water. It takes us four hours to cross the harbor and moor with difficulty between two yachts. As soon as we reach the quay, my first impulse is to jump ashore and greet the *Drenec,* a lovely forty-foot steel ketch: "If you've never seen a boat after it's turned over twice, now's your chance. You won't see it often."

We learn one boat is still drifting in the Gulf of Lions, her crew having abandoned her on Tuesday at the height of the storm. They sent out a distress signal and were rescued. And here is little Laurence drawing away beside me, giving lessons to her furry toy dog. It gives us pause.

12

Shipwrecked on the Banks
of the Ebro

We were all stricken with flu—luckily at two-day intervals, so that we could look after each other. We are all coughing, and still very low. But we're leaving Barcelona. Jean-Baptiste wants to get to Aguilas, to the south of Murcia, as quickly as possible. It was a question whether it would be better to leave now, ill as we are, with our crewmate, since it is already the end of November, or to wait until we are better, in mid-December, when our crew would have left and it would be colder and far more likely to be stormy. Our recent experience in the Gulf of Lions decides us to leave at once. Jean-Baptiste will take the tiller as much as he can.

I am chilled right through and worried about Laurence getting complications after her flu. We sleep together to try to keep each other warm, but she complains about not being able to turn over.

161

She likes watching the Barcelona-Valencia trains disappearing into the tunnels and coming out again, all the way down the coast. For the first time in all the years we've been sailing Christian has decided to keep within about five miles of shore, on the advice of the fishermen, because at this time of year the wind is mostly off the land, and if you want to sail in relatively calm waters you shouldn't go too far from the coast. We are making good speed and are glad to be sailing south.

"Mummy," Laurence says, "when we get to the beach, and the sea's warm, I'll swim with you." When we get to the beach. It makes me start worrying again about the life we are giving Laurence. But I think our way is better than the isolation of the Galápagos or the kind I myself experienced. But the way we live, after a spell on a desert island or at sea, we can rediscover the joys of city life—films, theaters, new books, new fashions; savor all the many reflections of the "spirit" of the times, and come in contact with the crowds—the crowds made up of thousands, each with his own history, his own story.

The child who lives on a boat has the advantage of life in the open air: a healthy, energetic, realistic existence, aware of life and death, survival, and also of civilization in all its stages—primitive, village life, city life. He will learn to integrate naturally into each. This is the true apprenticeship for our kind of happiness at sea. Besides the basic correspondence courses that his parents give him, he can also attend lessons for children of his own age for a month or so, to see how he measures up to them, and gain experience of group discipline, group activities, games, and art. Moreover, mixing with all sorts of different societies and social classes, he will learn the relative merits of customs and habits. He will see how each person earns his daily bread and compare the various ways in different countries.

I believe the greatest proof of love one can give a child is to teach him to be perfectly independent from the very beginning. To make him feel, practically from birth, that his happiness will come from his own efforts, the labors of his own hands. This means the parents must understand once and for all that the child is not theirs, is not their property. I don't find this very easy, and often have to reason with myself.

162

It begins as soon as the baby is born. A baby put down to lie on his back or side is absolutely dependent on his mother, and all his happiness comes from her. The same baby lying on his front sees the world quite differently. The first thing he can achieve for himself to give himself pleasure is to lift his head and cheek to one side or the other. He very quickly learns to crawl and then to climb on all fours—satisfactions which are quite independent of his mother. From the very first weeks he will know how to amuse himself, will become aware that it is he who chooses to amuse himself.

With a little patience you can easily teach a child to be absolutely independent by three years old. What a joy it was to see Laurence at that age put on a pretty dress when we arrived in port, jump ashore, and run to meet new friends. Or packing her little case to go and stay with friends for a week, who would be delighted to have a little thing of three who didn't wet her bed, could dress and wash herself, and who didn't make any extra work.

A self-sufficient child isn't the slave of his surroundings or his mother. You can work together on positive projects, because he's very mature. Not "old," but conscious of, and responsible for, his actions, like the little Polynesians who go off fishing at three years old, taking it very seriously. They aren't made stupid by being shouted at, or praised extravagantly for nothing. They are respected, as is their right, and they are very conscious of it.

It is this feeling of independence in the widest sense that I particularly liked about Laurence's correspondence school—*Pédagogie Moderne.* It teaches the child, from the age of three, to do things on his own. It educates the parents through their child—teaching them about happiness. There are endless good things from the child's point of view: practical projects and amusing tests, the chance of receiving a photocopy of work done by other children of the same age, and the pleasure of being corrected by someone other than Mummy. The child learns to enjoy studying by himself.

It's seven o'clock and we're listing more and more. At eight Jean-Baptiste goes on deck again. He says he's willing to do an eight-hour watch so we can get there more quickly. He and Christian consult the chart and the lights: to sail down the coast all you have to do is keep to the seaward side of all the beacons. The list

163

of lights, which is new, with corrections inserted, is spread on the table. The English chart is a year old—it's the most up-to-date of our four hundred pounds of charts.

Jean-Baptiste is at the helm; the wind is getting more and more violent, but the *Pygmalion* is riding smoothly. Passing the lights of Tarragona toward 1 A.M., we are very tempted to go into the harbor to spend the rest of the night. We think of all the people there, in the warmth. But it would be silly not to take advantage of this wind. We've already lingered too long in the Mediterranean. Tomorrow we'll be making for Alicante and it'll be hot. We sail on, leaving Tarragona behind.

2 A.M. Christian takes the helm. He is coughing a lot and comes below now and then to warm himself for a few minutes. From about three he stays on deck permanently. There's no moon. The sky is black, starless. The skipper stands farther out to sea. I'm always very scared at night in the Mediterranean because of all the boats. But it's even worse close to the shore. It's impossible to judge distances correctly. It was only the shock of capsizing, the flu, and the advice from the fishermen that made Christian take the risk. As if I had a presentiment, I say to Christian: "Luck doesn't last forever, you know."

At the end of Christian's watch, we can see a flashing light every two and a half seconds—Cape Tortosa, at the mouth of the Ebro. Christian goes back to bed, worn out and feverish, coughing more and more. Jean-Baptiste, at the tiller, keeps to the course set by Christian, out to sea. But the waves are building up and are coming from that direction. The boat is bucketing more and more and becoming uncomfortable. And our recent experience in the Gulf of Lions has made Jean-Baptiste wary. He's afraid of overturning again and steers closer to the wind in order to hug the coast more closely. Immediately it becomes more comfortable. Christian, exhausted by his fever, falls asleep like me, in spite of the howling of the wind in the rigging and the thundering of the waves. The *Pygmalion* flies along—Jean-Baptiste isn't worried. As he can see the beacon, a tiny light way off, quite clearly, there's no problem about going closer. Christian went too far out to sea during his watch and that was why we were buffeted about—it's more comfortable now.

And Christian recounts:

164

I had only been in bed half an hour when there was a jolt, not very bad, but quickly followed by others. We must be on a shoal. I rush out, yelling at Jean-Baptiste to leave the tiller and lower the jib—which he has never done before. He does so now at my command, letting the halyards fly while I throw myself at the anchor, cut it free and heave it overboard. What else could I do in the darkness? I know land is three hundred feet off. France, terrified, with Laurence in her arms, wants to send out an SOS rocket, launch the life raft. But I calm her. We wait below for the dawn.

Jean-Baptiste explains:

"We must be on a shoal, probably sand displaced by the Ebro, because the light's still a long way off. When we touched the first time, I thought it was just a little shoal and that we'd get off again. With this wind and going at the pace we were. So I kept the tiller in the same position. When the first waves hit us from astern, I realized we weren't moving. So I banged the tiller over, but Christian was already on deck."

In my arms Laurence says, "What a naughty sea, isn't it?" Poor little thing, sick, tired, only just recovered from capsizing. Frightening for a little four-year-old.

The waves hit us with terrible force, lifting our fifteen tons of steel and crashing us down with incredible violence. Both we and the hull tremble. We are all huddled in a ball on the floor of the saloon, clinging to each other as hard as we can and trying in vain not to be thrown about. Each blow bruises us more while threatening to break the masts. They're still holding.

Each time we're hit, we all strain our ears, waiting for the slow shuddering of the mast to stop. The hundred-pound anchor is torn from its place and wreaks havoc as it shifts about. In spite of his sore throat and the cold, Christian goes up to secure it. The close-reefed mizzen he set hasn't succeeded in turning us stern to the wind. He takes it down.

What can we do now? The shore is 330 feet off, bare, deserted, a sandy bog. What boat can come to aid us here, if we can't get off alone?

"The only thing to do," Christian says, "is to drop an anchor well to one side to make the boat heel over with the help of the main mast, so it will float in a little water. Then drop another

165

anchor, and haul us off with a pulley."

A gray dawn is breaking. The wind is still howling in the rigging. The rudder begins to bang loudly, being lifted on its hinges and crashed down again. The tiller is completely twisted.

As it grows light the sea redoubles in violence and the east wind increases. It's the worst possible wind for Cape Tortosa. We ought to wait till it dies down—but we have to try to get away from here. By eight it's broad daylight, and in spite of the overcast sky we can see that it's not an isolated sandbank in front of us, but quite simply the land, which stretches several kilometers beyond the light. Christian and Jean-Baptiste try every possible maneuver with the two anchors, but the wind and waves always drive us violently back toward shore, lifting up the *Pygmalion,* dumping her down closer inshore. We are stuck a few dozen yards from dead trees, which lift their bleached branches skyward.

What a comfort the steel hull is. "We're testing out the "Joshua" hull," Christian says laughing.

The interior is completely dry. But in spite of an incredible number of sweaters, trousers, tights, socks, jackets, and oilskins we're cold in our sleeping bags and blankets. We are still waiting for the sea to grow calmer, so that we can try some other way of getting off.

"I'm hungry, Mummy," Laurence says.

I get up painfully to heat some water. Standing in front of the stove, I automatically glance across to the beach opposite us.

"There's a man coming toward us, and two others behind him."

Jean-Baptiste leaps up and goes to meet them, struggling against the waves and the current, which threaten to carry him away.

They are fishermen. The boats from Ametlla de Mar caught sight of us early this morning. One of them apparently sailed over —some distance off, probably, because we didn't see or hear anything—but they couldn't see anyone. The fishermen in the Ebro also saw the *Pygmalion* at about seven o'clock. They came over at once. Seeing no one on board, they thought the boat had been abandoned. They reported it to the coast guard and the maritime authorities. They are now coming to make sure no one needs help.

166

Jean-Baptiste is the only one of us who speaks Spanish. The fishermen are very impressed to learn Laurence is on board. They insist that Jean-Baptiste persuade us to leave the boat before nightfall, because the wind and seas will come up again. The boat will be safe, they say, because of the sand. At the village we can get blankets, food, warmth, everything we need.

At first we don't want to leave *Pygmalion,* but finally, worn out by fever, sick, and tired, we agree. Jean-Baptiste takes a rope across to the beach, where the men hold it taut to make a lifeline for us. Laurence goes first, warmly dressed and wrapped up in her anorak with her inflated armbands, a life jacket round her waist and a security harness attached to Jean-Baptiste. As she's lowered toward the water she lets out a great howl, but then clings to Jean-Baptiste's shoulders and stops crying.

Once we arrive at the beach, a fisherman—Pantorilla—immediately wraps our little girl in a warm jacket, and stays beside her, not leaving her till evening, helping us untiringly. On board, we each pack a bag: besides my few indispensable clothes, the ship's papers and our personal papers, I put in a packet of candy, a green plush tortoise, and my movie camera. Jean-Baptiste makes two journeys with the waterproof bags, while Christian continues to lash down anything that might get broken or spoiled. In the exodus-like atmosphere, we leave all our most precious things on board: navigation equipment, radio, tape recorder, binoculars, photographs—all our treasures.

The coast guard commander tells us that since the mouth of the Ebro has shifted from east to west and the beacon was moved, we are the fourth yacht in a year to go aground on the same spot. It's disgraceful the beacon should be so far inland and that there isn't another light. The sand, which is on a level with the water, is so difficult to distinguish, either in daylight or at night, because there is no vegetation, no houses, no lights. At least they could put a light buoy there. The worst is that the concrete base of the old light is still there, sticking up about six feet. If we had been three hundred feet nearer, we would have been dashed against it.

Christian finally leaves his boat, after having made a last tour of the deck, shutting the hatch securely, swallowing his disappointment. He must be remembering his titanic labors building his dear

167

two-masted *Pygmalion* alone, in Marseille, in the icy cold. He's completely crushed.

The fishermen don't talk much. They too are thoughtful. One of them says that the last yachtsmen to get stuck there had to wait for three days for the wind to go down, before he could get his boat off. Three days. It seems like an eternity to us.

We walk forty long minutes across the wet sand, pitted with marram grass, across marshland, where a herd of small black cows with long, sharp, curling horns are feeding. Sinister gray sand— absolutely deserted. Not a house, not a person in sight. Only great trunks of dead trees washed down by the Ebro over the whole stretch of land, several miles in length, dead level with the water.

A long, sad journey taking us farther and farther from the *Pygmalion.* Our feet sink in up to the ankles; most of the way we're walking in water. We turn around from time to time to look at the boat. She's still there. But we can't tell how she's doing now; we aren't there to come to her aid if something breaks. All we can do is come back helplessly to see what harm's been done, our hearts heavy at having left her to be battered to pieces alone.

We reach the mouth of the Ebro at last. Pantorilla's motorboat is tied to a decrepit landing stage. We all get in and are across the Ebro in a few minutes. Jean-Baptiste has great difficulty in interpreting for us, because we are in a very isolated part of Spain, where they speak a barely comprehensible Catalan.

The coast guard commander suggests taking us to an inn in the village ten miles away. We'll be quite comfortable there until the weather improves. Then he'll ask in Amettla port for volunteers to come and haul us off with their big fishing boats. We can hardly spend the last of our money now. Especially when it means going ten miles away, with no means of getting from the village to the boat.

The fishermen listen in silence. When I turn to look for Laurence, they point to a little fisherman's hut at the edge of the water. "We don't like to offer you such a poor hut," the fishermen say. "But if it's any help you can stay there as long as you like. There are rice, fish, wine."

It seems like a castle to us. It's just what we need and it is we who feel embarrassed at accepting so much kindness. The hut is twelve by fifteen feet, built of whitewashed brick and weather-beaten. There is a little chimney, and a large bed of planks covered with dried furze is on the earth floor. Four stools, a table, two shelves, and a tank for drinking water. The doorway opens toward the Ebro. Two little windows look over the river and toward the boat; you can see the *Pygmalion*—a tiny speck on the horizon. The commander leaves his binoculars so we can keep an eye on her. Pantorilla takes a list of what we need from the village for the night. A fisherman gives us some fish, which we grill over the fire with some potatoes. We have all we need to be content. By eight we're all asleep.

Sunday, November 28, 1971. The sun is shining and the sky's blue, but the wind and waves are still squally. The *Pygmalion* is still shifting, being knocked from side to side. Christian is longing to go back to her, but no one wants to go with him: the current is very strong in the Ebro and one would need a powerful motorboat to cross. There are only rowboats here today. The commander promises some trawlers to tow us off when the weather gets better. With everyone around us helping there is a great feeling of togetherness.

Laurence plunges into all the delights of the countryside. A gray donkey is her great joy, two sheepdogs her first loves: she strokes them and presses her face against theirs. Then she follows the movements of the herd of little black cows in the neighboring marsh.

Tonight we're assessing the situation. We can hear wild ducks calling in the darkness. The Ebro delta is a famous shooting ground for wild fowl. And the next day we can't wait any longer; Christian and I decide to go to the boat, leaving Laurence in the hut with Jean-Baptiste. A fisherman lends us a boat. The current and wind carry us off course, and we have to row hard. We tie the boat up on the opposite bank, and set off on our way to the *Pygmalion* in our diving suits.

The boat hasn't moved much. She has dug herself a trough, in which she is still rocking. Around this hollow the water comes halfway up our calves. It will be very difficult getting her out of there, and it's depressing when we know there's no tide. Nothing has moved inside. What a relief. We can't help remembering that this is all we possess. Feeling more and more like shipwrecked sailors, we bundle up more warm clothes, blankets, sleeping bags. We bring the guitar, some games, and school books for Laurence.

Going back across the Ebro, we have to struggle against the current and the wind. We realize why the boats always have two or three oarsmen. The oars are so heavy I can use only one at a time.

The next day we see all the trawlers from Ametlla go out about twelve miles beyond the *Pygmalion*—but there's still no word from the commander. The fishermen repeat that they are entirely at our disposal, that they are only waiting for the green light from the commander to act. Meanwhile they give us fish every day. There's no wind tonight, and the sea has gone down—if only this weather lasts. The sun has set. On the horizon we can see the boat in the sand, then more sand, which looks very black in this light, and the dark marshes, above which fly hundreds of gulls and wild ducks in arrow formation. Then some ruined houses, more black sand and the island of Buda, a strip of land planted with poplars, which are darkly silhouetted against the sun, setting in a pinky orange streak across the horizon. On the other side the hazy blue *sierras* gradually melt into the darkness. The beacon—the wretched landlocked beacon—sends out its wrecker's rays.

The wind comes up in the night and blows more and more strongly. Damn! Yesterday we could have . . . And today, of course, in this wind, there's no commander.

We've been here five days already.

I do a few *Pédagogie Moderne* kindergarten lessons with Laurence. They can be endlessly adapted. Yesterday she drew the stranded boat and everything she has collected on the beach. Most of the day is spent in games of observation. This morning she caught her first frog. When she's played with the little creature for a while, I say: "You must put it back in the water now. Otherwise its Daddy and Mummy will be worried."

After a minute or two one of the fishermen comes up. "Your little girl keeps asking us to catch the Daddy and Mummy frogs." I should have thought of that.

In the evening it starts pouring rain. I hurriedly gather some dry wood. Tomorrow morning four trawlers are supposed to be

170

coming to tow us out. We feel very nervous. I keep thinking that $100 is almost all we have left. And two more days pass: too much wind and rain.

In the afternoon several people visit us, including Pantorilla and his wife, who bring us two loaves. This morning Felix gave us three ducks' eggs and some fruit jelly for Laurence. How kind they are. Laurence has a visit from one of her dog friends, his fur dripping with water. The wind howls the whole day and all through the night, while the rain pours down. It soaks our pillows and part of the floor, drowning the fire. It's so cold we can't get to sleep again.

Another day. The fishermen come very early this morning, because the current flowing down the Ebro appears to have vanished. The waves are pushing upriver. The men have their boats out, but they are swamped, as if the Ebro were suddenly twice as large as usual. The little jetty opposite the hut has disappeared under the water. As soon as we go outside the water comes up to our knees, and it's seeping into the hut everywhere. Going out to get some wood, I get my last pair of socks wet. My feet are frozen. Some fishermen are vainly trying to haul up a net, which they put out yesterday, because the branches being washed downriver are tearing the nets.

An Ebro fisherman's life is a hard one. They don't get much for their fish. Every day they spend the whole morning cleaning the net they put out the evening before, often for only one basket of fish. The only rewarding fishing is for young eels, just a few inches long and transparent. They are a great delicacy and very expensive. That is the reason our hut is there. The fishermen use very fine nets, in the shape of a cage, which are anchored to the end of the little jetty now under water. A small kerosene lamp is installed on the jetty to attract the eels on moonless nights.

The wind is so strong that it's very difficult to open the door. The beacon is in a lake, and the visibility is so poor that at eleven in the morning we can't see the boat even with the binoculars. There's obviously no point in getting in touch with the fishermen in Ametlla. We'll have to wait till tomorrow.

More days pass, and it gets worse and worse. The boat is digging in more deeply and we are increasingly rundown. We have

171

flu again. But what can we do other than wait until we can get the boat off? We'll do it if it kills us.

The oldest fisherman brings us some potatoes, rice, parsley, and garlic. Two of them rowed over from the other bank, in spite of the rain, wind, and cold. How generous they are! We have never asked them for anything. Both blessings and miseries seem to rain down on us.

The fire refuses to light, but Laurence is still very cheerful, playing all day long. It will soon be Christmas and we're making things in preparation, with the help of her little school.

A sudden commotion: the mayor of La Cava, a very young, friendly, dynamic man, arrives in a Land-Rover with a guard.

"Bring your things—I'm taking you to La Cava. When you are famous you will be able to tell everyone that there's a very nice little village in Spain."

We leave some of our things in the hut, with the bedding, and just take a small bag. There's so much water everywhere that it's like driving through the sea. On the way to La Cava we see only rice fields on every side, with pink flamingoes and white herons that have come to feed.

In the village, the landlord of a café pension, the 21 Bar, gives us a drink. He tells us a room is all ready for us, and that we can have all our meals there. We can ask him for anything we need and we mustn't worry about anything: the mayor and he will take care of it all.

And then a beautiful *paella* is laid before us, without our asking, with some soup for Laurence. A real house, with dry floors —we can't believe our eyes. Laurence plays with a caged owl. It seems that there has never been weather like this within living memory. We couldn't have chosen a worse moment to run aground. It seems there is nothing we can do, and so it is pointless to worry about being a bit farther from the boat. We must gather our strength—we'll need it.

13

Afloat Again

José and Regina, the owners of the café, have a little boy of six, José. They treat us like members of the family. And how well we slept that night between clean sheets.

The days pass; we go on making plans. The weather is no better, with wind every day. None of the fishing boats would risk sailing closer even if the wind dropped a bit, or even if there were only a few small waves, because they need a perfectly calm, clear sea—summer weather in fact. But it won't be summer for a long while yet.

Laurence is completely happy. Her life is full of excitements. She plays in the café and is given cakes and candy and chewing gum —which she enjoys all the more because she knows we thoroughly disapprove. The only stable element in her life is the little school,

173

with which we persevere no matter what happens. She goes out with her friend José, and goes shopping with him. She's very independent and spends as little time with us as possible.

We'll never get off. The *Pygmalion* has been stranded on the sand for three weeks now. As in a nightmare, each move seems thwarted, doomed before it starts. We now know that the famous trawlers will need a whole day to tow us off; they can only come on a Sunday, so that they won't lose a day's work. Which is reasonable. If the weather's not good on a Sunday, but on a week day, the sardine fishermen will come, because they work at night. But they have far less powerful engines. If it means hauling with a windlass, there's a big difference between theirs and the trawlers'. On the other hand they draw far less water and could get nearer the *Pygmalion*.

We are in a very embarrassing position, because we're receiving help from all sides: the mayor of La Cava and the 21 Bar are keeping us, the Tortosa commander is doing all he can, and the fishermen . . . If it weren't for them we would have to go back and live on the boat until our stores ran out, fishing every day and trying our utmost to rescue the *Pygmalion*.

We spend Christmas in Barcelona with the Zendrera family. Although we barely knew them at first, they have become like a family to us. No one could imagine how much they did for us after the shipwreck. They are the most generous people. The house is warm and comfortable, but the most restful thing about it is the calm atmosphere, even though there are never fewer than ten or twelve people there (they have eight children). But everyone is treated with great respect and love—a real family community. And we have a real family Christmas.

The streets of Barcelona smell of Christmas. It would be wonderful to be able to buy presents for all our friends.

After a month of waiting, uncertainty, and false starts, we decide to empty the boat and strip out her ballasts, no easy task.

At the 21 Bar we continue to mull over possible ways of towing off the boat. We could dig a channel through the sand, about 250 feet long, from the boat to the Ebro River—with a dredger. But how would we get a dredger?

174

The boat is so much lighter once the ballast has been removed that she's floating already in the hole she has dug. Then she moves onto the sand, toward the sea. She's out of the hole and in two feet of water—she's moving. It looks as though it would be easy to tow her off with the fishing boats now. But there's a bank of sand four hundred feet farther on, before she gets to the sea. Can she get over it?

A sardine boat is coming to tow us off.

Today it's overcast. There's no wind. The sea is flat and calm. After much maneuvering, the towing begins. The men are all in the icy water in their wet suits. After an hour the *Pygmalion* has moved a few inches according to the guide marks. It's not much; she may have simply turned a bit. But at least she's moving, and our hopes revive. It's like seeing a person move whom one is afraid may be dying—it suddenly gives you renewed hope.

We're still there as it grows dark. We make a huge fire on the beach, while the sardine boat struggles to haul up its anchor. No one has had anything to eat. We go slowly back to the hut in the pitch darkness, the only lights the blinking one-eyed beacon and the tiny kerosene lamp for the eels on the jetty by the hut.

Our valiant rescuers, Paco, Tomas, Carlos, and Ushi, have a celebration dinner at the 21 Bar with us. They make a huge *cara-chillo*—flambéing some cognac with thyme and rosemary in an earthenware bowl. Then you add a little cinnamon and drink it hot or mixed with boiling hot black coffee. The men are sleeping at the 21 Bar because tomorrow we're going to tow the *Pygmalion* again, but this time with some tractors from the island of Buda.

Ten o'clock. After several setbacks the tractors arrive. Unfortunately there's a north wind again, and in spite of the sun it's arctic. The sea has built up and there's a current. We make our first attempt, with one tractor alone. The boat doesn't budge, even when the pulleys get closer together. The *Pygmalion* only turns round a bit. It takes a good half hour to put the tackle back in place. The wind redoubles in strength and sand gets in everything, even in the plastic bags our sandwiches are in. Paco wants to stop and so does Tomas.

On the beach our nerves are stretched to breaking point. We thought it would be so easy, that the boat would continue to move.

But no one dares leave, for Christian is still determined to go on trying and not wait for a day when it's calmer. At two o'clock we make our second and final attempt. Without success. The tractors leave.

The agent on Buda Island lends them to us again two days later. At the first attempt the line to the tractor breaks. There's no wind. It's hot. Second attempt: The four-hundred-pound anchor gives. Third attempt: Some sacks filled with sand have been hung on the mast to make the boat heel over as much as possible. And the boys hang on to the sacks, to give extra weight. The boat shifts a few inches but the anchor still comes away. So all the other anchors are added to it—with no success. The Tortosa commander will send his trawlers on Sunday. But on Sunday it's raining, the sky is overcast, and although there's no wind they would never dare come to the Ebro in this weather.

At about eleven Carlos arrives with Ushi and some friends. He's distraught because the sea is quite calm, higher than he's ever seen it in seventeen years, and the trawlers aren't here. We can see what happens with binoculars from the hut, in spite of the rain, and watch as the *Pygmalion* visibly begins to float, and then as she moves several feet toward the Ebro River. Then she turns right round on herself—it's magnificent. It's one o'clock—the *Pygmalion* is in the river, floating free and rolling dreadfully because there's no ballast —*she's off the sand.* It's fantastic to see her floating again after two months on the sand, on a rainy day, when no other boat wanted to come—when the sea was higher than it had ever been before. Delirious excitement at the 21 Bar. We fall hungrily on a giant paella.

After having been reballasted, scraped, repaired, painted, and repainted, the *Pygmalion* is our home again, and in May we set out to sea. We spend the summer in the Balearics, and Laurence's little sister, Mareva, is born on October 28 in Barcelona. While she is being introduced to life amid the smell of pine trees, rosemary, thyme, and lavender, Christian sails solo across the Atlantic. He has decided to sell the *Pygmalion* and build the perfect yacht, the yacht of his dreams.

176

14

Alone Across the Atlantic: Christian's Letters to France

I go with the wind, people of Orphalese,
but not down into emptiness;
—The Prophet

Arrecife, November 23

You must be thinking that I'm alone in the middle of the Atlantic, but I'm not, because the splendid northeast wind that brought me here has vanished and I'd rather wait in harbor until it returns than wait at sea or use the engine, while I'm alone. . . .

I keep asking myself a thousand questions about the future. The years are flying past—the years when we can walk naked along deserted beaches on sun-drenched islands.

I love my boat so much. Yesterday I spent six hours putting a net around the stays to stop the flying fish from getting back to the water—today an hour washing down the hull. I don't even know whether anyone will sell me a bare plastic hull, or how much

177

it would cost. One needs a lot of courage and optimism to think of starting all over again.

Las Palmas, November 28

I envy you at heart for being on dry land, on sweet-smelling earth. Especially as I'm going mad alone on board without any social contact. The crossing is assuming proportions that it never would have if you were with me. A month alone at sea, in this great boat: the last crossing was bad enough.

I was burning with impatience at Arrecife, waiting for the wind, and suddenly left on the spur of the moment, on Sunday morning, without any provisions, telling myself that I could call in at Las Palmas on the way to get in some supplies. I ran into a dead calm a few minutes after leaving, although I had set sail with a good wind. I started the engine and decided to call in at Lobos, a little island between Fuerteventura and Lanzarote.

Four boats moored alongside the *Pygmalion;* barbecue on the beach; back on board and off to sleep after my long day.

In the middle of the night the wind came up on the least-protected side. The mooring became impossible, with the wind blowing harder and harder. I got dressed, hauled in the anchor, stowed everything away, and started the engine preparatory to leaving. Day broke, gray and uninviting, the barometer very low, and we all decided to leave for Las Palmas in the evening, in order to arrive by daylight, as it's ninety-five miles away.

And there was *Pygmalion* with her sails set, wind astern, waiting for the two others to start, and then flying along at nine knots like some fantastic horse, with the automatic pilot. We overtook the other two boats and lost them from sight. And one of them was doing twelve knots—a racing yacht that had won at several regattas.

Then it was night, pitch dark and with a strong breeze. The Coleman lantern lit up the boat beautifully but blinded me, so I couldn't even see thirty feet ahead. What a marvelous night. By 2 A.M. I could see Las Palmas. By five I was entering the harbor. Ninety-five miles in twelve hours. And, in spite of the wind, I would have had a good night's sleep if there had been no land ahead.

178

So—got in supplies and up and off. My heart in my boots at not having you with me to tackle the Atlantic. It will be a long month.

Pygmalion, December 4

I'm writing this letter in mid-Atlantic, having left Las Palmas four days ago, alone with *Pygmalion*. There was a strong breeze and the sky was gray, but I was longing to get on with it, to see you again. My friends in the boats moored all around sounded their sirens and wished me *bon voyage* as I set sail in spectacular style.

Four days. The barometer and winds are fine, but I'm not. It's sad being alone, especially when I know there are three marvelous little women waiting for me in Spain. The days and nights seem endless. I don't go on deck much—only for a few minutes every day. I've only taken one sight since I left to check my course. I'm not particularly hungry or physically tired, but am not sleeping very well.

You don't realize in harbor how long a month can be. Luckily *Pygmalion*'s making good speed, 160 miles a day at least, on average (185 miles the first day), but I always have the same problem with the sail, sailing before the wind: the jibs are screened by the mizzen and mainsail. If I change tack and sail on a broad reach, I get off course, one way or the other. So I am taking it more slowly, without the jib, with mainsail and mizzen goosewinged.

I hope to arrive in Amettla before this letter, but it does me good to write to you. If only we could spend Christmas together. But I'm not looking forward to being cold again; I'm just reaching the sun. I'm naked, believe it or not, and the sun gets hotter every day.

December 4

A good night. Toward midnight the wind strengthened and veered to the east, so I'm sailing off the wind with all the sails set. The speedometer has stuck at nine and there are often spurts at ten or even eleven knots. But it can only be relied on up to ten. Six hundred twenty miles in four days—not too bad. If I continue at this rate I'll be across in under twenty days.

179

So last night I put her on course again, and changed bunks because we're listing a bit now, and squeezed a lemon over my head. My hair had been looking very sad—it did it good. Then I rinsed it in the dark in salt water, on deck. I'm longing for the sun to be hot enough to have a good wash on deck. Anyway I'm running at high speed toward the south, the Equator.

I'll have to take my bearings for the second time in four days because I said 620 miles, but that's by the log. With a one-and-a-half-knot current I must have done much more.

Why am I not a forester instead of a sailor? I could at least see our little Mareva feeding and smiling in your arms. I'm a bit worried in case you leave her with Laurence, who might pick her up while you're out—accidents can happen so quickly.

I'm looking at the speedometer dial as I write: we're doing ten knots practically all the time. One needs a log speedometer graduated from one to fifteen. But the wind isn't all that strong because I have all the sails set, and am writing below. It's force five or six. It's really terrific and I'd like it to stay like this all the way.

The refrigerator's not working. I got in a lot of fresh meat: a two-pound roast, a pound of fillet steak, ten slices of ham and a chicken. The joint was already smelling a bit yesterday when I put it in the pan.

What a pity I don't have a camera with me. I keep thinking what a voyage like this means. A desert 3,700 miles wide, without an oasis; alone on a machine made of fifteen tons of steel, driven by wind and storm.

4:30. You've no idea how long the days seem. I can't stay lying down; it makes me feel queasy all over. But there's quite a swell and I ought to be tired. I listened to France-Inter this afternoon on my new transistor—that did me good. It was a program about toys for handicapped children. Will we be together for Christmas? I hope so very much.

The pan's steaming away with all the meat in it, and some diced vegetables, unpeeled. I only give the Primus a run once a day.

While it's cooking I'm making an enormous salad that you wouldn't get ashore: apples, bananas, greens, tomatoes, almonds, dried raisins, onions, peanut butter, olive oil, lemon, olives, peppers, and oranges.

180

I make a ritual of a few things that keep me sane, because it's enough to drive you crazy, you know, to be alone on a boat for so long. I haul up the line once a day (of course the spoon's gone and I had to put on a new one). While up there I saw my first flying fish.

Then I cooked my hot meal. Then checked our position. I went up a little too early for the latitude and had to wait half an hour until the sun started to get lower. I have put a compass in the middle of the saloon and I have to get up from time to time to adjust our course a little, but not often. And you only have to give a pull to alter it five degrees. No maneuvering with the sails at the moment —hope it lasts like that. Of course all the seams of the mainsail have given where it rubs against the shroud but I'm leaving them like that until I get to the Antilles.

I'm having great difficulty keeping my hand steady while writing.

4 A.M. Three fish on deck. They couldn't escape because of the net I put up at Arrecife.

What a shame to be passing so close to the Cape Verde Islands without calling in there. I sometimes think I might just put this letter on a yacht, without dropping anchor or lowering the sails.

Las Palmas hasn't changed at all since we were last there, except that this time I didn't moor alongside all the other boats at the end of the harbor, but in the open water opposite the yacht club, and I also signed the visitors' book. There were several other boats there and the water was clean. If I wanted to go to the market I just chugged across the harbor. . . .

I'm writing all this in mid-Atlantic. The miles flash past at nine or ten knots (but never quickly enough for me), and I've already done 760 miles. If I do an average of 160 miles a day, I'll be across in eighteen or twenty days: not long enough for my beard to grow. Ah—these fast boats.

I notice I'm hardly touching my reserve of drinking water. I only need a little Coca-Cola, a little fresh milk, or some fruit.

5 A.M. I'm going to sleep for a while. Good night, my love.

8 A.M. I dreamed, so I must have been asleep. I had left you on board with Laurence while I went to get the mail, with the boat gently drifting along a river. When I got back the boat wasn't there. I found it at last; you were on land and I had great difficulty tacking against the current, which had gotten stronger. . . .

It's gray and gloomy, with a strong wind. When will I be able to wash myself in the boiling sun? I'm rather miserable at the moment, like someone with an incurable illness teetering toward death.

I'm not even bothering to navigate; the boat's doing all the work. I just glance vaguely at the compass to see that we're going more or less toward the west, and pull a bit of rope from time to time.

5 P.M., December 5

My fifth day at sea. I'm past the Cape Verde Islands. I could almost see them, sixty miles away on the port side, but it's still just as gray and windy, the barometer's low, and it's all rather gloomy. It's a great strain on the nerves. . . .

Let's go live on a farm. But I need a climate where I can go naked all year. That means Polynesia. But how old will we be before we get there again? Look what's become of my log book: a long letter to my dear wife.

If you could see the interior of the *Pygmalion*—utter chaos. And what I look like. I'm going to have a blitz and clean up everything. Only five days. I'll never get there. But the log says 840 miles, thank goodness. Tomorrow I'll have done a third of the voyage in six days. I'm not particularly trying to go fast. I haven't the means. You would need two large booms and two genoa sails, or a spinnaker and a square gaff sail. Not a mizzen, in fact, which takes the wind from the mainsail as soon as you're on course (running before the wind), and a mainsail, which takes it from the jibs. But I've proved several times since Casablanca that the *Pygmalion* is going very fast, passing racing yachts of her own size.

5. P.M. There are six pounds of meat (roast and steak) cooking in the pan because they were beginning to spoil. It's the second or third time they've been cooked. The first time, with no water, the roast was delicious—pink and tender. The next day I added the steak, which was smelling a bit, and made it all into stew, also very good, but today it was a bit tough.

182

I'd like to do the whole voyage without opening any cans, but I haven't got enough vegetables and fruit. I'm sick of the cheese, although they're very good—goat's, Dutch, Roquefort, and Gruyère—and usually choose the meat. Tomorrow I'll have my stew again, and my first avocados (bought unripe). The bananas, peppers, and pears are finished. The oranges would have lasted, but there are only twelve left. I still have ten pounds of onions, twenty of potatoes—and I'll soon be on rice and corned beef. The peppers are rapidly withering, and the eggplants have had it. . . .

6 P.M. The day is passing very slowly: the mizzen is flapping; the staysail is set badly, so I have regulated Gigi a bit. The trade wind seems much stronger than the one we had. I haven't seen any dorados, probably because I'm always down below. And the spoon on the fishing line's no good: it twists and jumps out of the water and gets tangled up—and we're going too fast. . . .

Meanwhile, my pen's giving out and we're rolling, rolling, under a black sky, and the barometer's falling. Now I really feel I'm battling with the Atlantic. Another two thousand miles and we're there.

How I long to see my little Mareva. There are thousands of questions I want to ask and I do hope there'll be a long letter from you when I get to Barbados. And you will never have had such a long one as mine to you. I didn't make the crossing direct from Tangier, although the winds were favorable, because I couldn't resist the temptation of seeing Casablanca and the Canaries. So we will have been apart for two months. When will we at last have a real married life? Time passes so quickly. New Zealand, the instant-photograph interlude, our voyage on the *Alpha,* a year in Tahiti, construction of the *Pygmalion,* sailing lessons in Greece, shipwreck, winter in Spain, Mareva, separated again—what a life!

Oh, well, only a few more days and I can look forward to seeing you again, as lovely as the evening when you arrived in Palma this summer.

I've found a pen! and will leave you for a minute to go and eat a raw tomato with mayonnaise, with a cup of hibiscus tea with honey which I put in the Thermos. God—it's really rolling now.

Good morning, madam. I've just gotten up. Chaos reigns here, although I could soon clean it up: all the Arabian cushions are spread on my two mattresses on the floor, with the radio, compass, some books and magazines that I always leave lying around, a bottle of Coca-Cola, the amplifier, a box of cornflakes—that's all in the saloon. The kitchen is filthy.

Did I wake up in the night? Yes, feeling a bit sick. Where is that healthy third-day feeling? I ate an orange and drank a little dried milk in water, which did the trick. But my stomach is churning madly. I don't know if it's muscular, because of the movement of the boat, or because of my poor diet or all the worry recently, but it really hurts when we roll. I don't want to end up with a stomach ulcer.

Often at night, almost every night, I have lovely dreams; I'm on land again, and suddenly I wake up and it takes me a few minutes to realize where I am. It's so disappointing to hear nothing but the waves, the water rushing past the hull, to be bucketing along in this tub, for weeks yet, when five days already seem like an eternity. But this morning I feel more hopeful because the log says 950 miles, which is a third of the way, and I can look forward to getting there. Hot baths, swimming, sun. Even if it's only for a day or two it will do me good. Best of all would be if you could join me with the girls.

The wind has strengthened and the speedometer reads nine knots: with only half the sails set that's pretty good. Not so good was a vicious wave that attacked the boat and drenched the after cabin. I had put the cheese and other food on the floor: all that plus the carpet got a bath.

Did I tell you about Morocco? Tangier first—you'd adore the Medina, which is all sloping streets, with beautiful dresses, very cheap. I was longing to be there with you and buy everything.

The Casa yacht club has many more boats, but it doesn't have the same friendly atmosphere as before.

December 6. Midday by my watch, which is still on Greenwich Mean Time. In fact it will be midday in two hours' time because I've already gone 30 degrees west, and it's one hour for 15 degrees. So in two hours' time I'll go and take my noon sight. Meanwhile the fix I have just taken puts me too far to the south again. I can't seem to head for the West Indies. But I see why: 20 degrees magnetic variation, 20 degrees compass deviation from the steel deck. To steer west (270) I must steer 310 by the compass. One would have to steer 330 if one were sailing on the wind (drifting), almost due north by the compass to steer a true westerly course.

I'll see what tomorrow's sights will say about my corrections.

3 P.M. I'm getting the upper hand. Average since we left: 160 miles a day, which means eighteen days for the crossing, so I'll be there in twelve days.

The wind's dropping, and the sky's getting bluer, and it's marvelous to feel the sun on me again.

What a lot I've done since I got up: I haven't lain down for an instant. Changed the fishing line, long session taking bearings, a little tidying up, cooked and ate stew. Listened to some good music on my mini-cassettes: Carol King, Cat Stevens, James Taylor.

5:30. The sun will soon be setting. I read some articles in my sailing magazines, and suddenly remembered the avocados: just ripe. It's a shame they all get ripe together because I'll soon be sick of them. My first one, which I ate just as the log came up to 1,000 miles (the log's an optimist!), was delicious. In fact I've only done 950 miles in a direct line. If I subtract the boat's "deviations" and little excursions, there must still be an error of 5 percent.

8:30. The sun's set on my sixth day at sea. I stayed on deck quite a while and changed course: now I'm sailing toward the sun. The *Nautical Almanac* gives the bearing at sunset (263 degrees today). So if I go a little more "to the right," I'll reach Barbados in a few days. It was good on deck. The wind's dropped a lot. The Spanish courtesy flag, which I haven't taken down, is flapping gently, but *Pygmalion*'s still making good headway, and waves that look impressive to some people, but that I find exciting—which I adore in fact—send us surf riding.

The loneliness is enough to make you hysterical. For a start you forget how to talk, and find yourself yelling in order to hear yourself and break the silence, or looking quickly behind you to see if there's a giant octopus tentacle. But that isn't the real danger, I know. It's during the long nights asleep when the boat could run smack into a steel wreck, which would pierce the waterline, and it would all be over in a few seconds. Perhaps not even time to launch the life raft. And what about water, clothes, tins of food? You'd drift for months, toward almost certain death.

December 7

(In ten days I shall be sadly spending my birthday alone at sea.) A fine calm night. Cloudy and more wind this morning, but not as much as the first few days. We're only doing seven knots. I cooked my first hot breakfast: hot chocolate, eggs, and bacon. But I'm scared of getting food poisoning from this flabby bacon from the warm refrigerator, although it doesn't smell bad.

Still no luck with the line. This time it's a plastic bottle on the hook. But I have enough meat at present. And there are some flying fish on the deck. And the eggs, which I haven't felt like for weeks, are still perfectly fresh, as I discovered this morning. Did you drink the hibiscus tea I left you? I've just made myself a Thermosful, sweetened with honey from Amettla de Mar. It's delicious and reminds me of our holidays.

What an exciting moment going down with the figures and sextant, and tracing a new cross on the chart (only 140 miles today, our worst day; if the *Alpha* could hear that!). At last it's warm enough not to wear any clothes. The waves are much smaller so that sometimes, when I'm lying in the saloon on my Moroccan cushions with a newspaper and music to drown the noises outside, the motion is so slight, even at eight knots, that I wonder if I'm really alone on the *Pygmalion* in the middle of the Atlantic.

Seventh day gone. Still averaging 160 miles a day, and maybe I'll be across in twenty.

December 8

These days alone are a good retreat. It's six here, and the sun's just rising. *Pygmalion*'s going like a real steamer: steady course, little movement, constant speed, and her only passenger, captain, cook, maître d'hôtel, radio officer, etc., is finding time passing very slowly. But as I get in better physical shape I'm beginning to get a lot out of this time alone and have no regrets. . . .

186

I haven't yet shaken off the effect of the staggering story of Captain Scott's expedition to the South Pole: I've just heard it in the dark, on a tape recording. They all died, eleven miles from the camp, on the way back. They found his diary in the tent where they were waiting for the storm to pass before doing the last few miles. With only one day's provisions and a temperature of minus forty degrees, they must have suffered terribly.

I hope you're keeping snug in your little house and not having any doubts about the future, our future.

1:30 A.M. I'm at it again—dreaming about boats. My dreams get more and more fantastic, and the Morgan hull haunts me—even if it takes all my money. It would at least be a floating roof. The rest would follow in due course. A mast, two sails, a bit of wood. Providing they'll do it. And we'll build it at Russ's. It would be really good in Florida too, because of the climate.

What a fantastic adventure, really: 3,750 miles across the sea at six or seven miles an hour, alone, with no pollution, no talking. You will know that I'm feeling much better. I needed this retreat. And really, in spite of everything, I'm enjoying this voyage a lot. And I'd like to be in top form when I arrive because my plans for the future will need a lot of energy, to make up for lack of money.

I go on writing and writing but none of it is reaching you, and I wonder if you're bearing up all right. It's good to write to someone you have complete confidence in, whom you love and to whom you want to give everything; it's better than just thinking about her, I feel closer writing and make a little more effort.

Naturally I'd rather be making love on a sunny desert island than scribbling these lines. Wouldn't you?

Pygmalion gallops along majestically. Soft, regular, musical movements; my steed forges on, eating up the miles, tirelessly. Along her flanks, the water rushes, sparkles, gleams in phosphorescent spray; her bow cuts through the dark night. *Pygmalion* glories in her speed, and to make her pleasure last, crosses the vast ocean without haste.

Yes, well, spontaneity is a fine thing but writing is like swimming: You need to work hard before you get it right. It's a game, an art, this wielding of pen or words.

Oh time! suspend your flight; and you,
    auspicious hours!
Stay a while:
Let us savor the fleeting delights
Of these happiest of our days!

Tonight I'm happy to be alone in the middle of the Atlantic on this boat I built myself, which I know utterly, like my body, with all its faults and qualities; which resembles me; which I love.

I put the light out and dive into the cushions and under my sleeping bag and don't dare look at the small bright square in the ceiling—the hole of the hatch opening to the outside world. I can see the huge tentacle of a giant octopus coming in and slowly wavering toward me to seize me and squash me between its suckers and carry me off to the bottom of the ocean. I shut my eyes, pull myself together, and don't think about it, but there are odd noises —is someone on board? How could he be? And yet . . . I don't dare get up.

Now I've come to write these few words to you by the light of the torch, hurriedly, before going to sleep.

3 A.M. No. I'm still not asleep, so you can have the benefit of my lyricism again. Too many things have been running through my head during this hour in the dark. I was thinking that man is basically good. In what connection? Telling myself that tomorrow I would make some pastry. No—I've hundreds of more important things to do to make myself feel good: wash myself all over, clean the boat.

Everyone dreams of being happy. If I don't do this or that, it's because I haven't the strength.

No drugs on board: no coffee, tea, tobacco, alcohol, medicines, nothing. How nice. And I think every orgasm, whether physical or intellectual, sublimated or not, which you achieve with the help of these drugs lowers the threshold of the one you have the next time without them. Drugs make people impotent—impotent people have need of drugs.

Blow, whistle, blow! From below I hear a rumbling: a wave comes, lifts the stern, *Pygmalion* goes up, up; it eddies, she rides on the surf; it's terrifying; she comes almost broadside to slide down

188

more slowly and then rests for two or three seconds. The wind takes over, fills the white canvas to bursting point; everything strains, trembles, we are taking wing, but *Pygmalion* likes swimming. A new mountain comes up behind us, high, swift but calm, lifts her gently, grows, up and up, faster and faster, then bursts, foaming with happiness.

3:30. You can get excited without drinking coffee, you see. I stay on deck for a minute; it's so lovely—words would spoil it. Yet I'd rather come below to write you than go on looking. What a marvelous night; the wind is tireless, cool, but good on my bare body. The stars have never seemed so close, so alive, their light so soft, like the ceiling of my vast palace. The pole star, very low, well to starboard, shows me I am going due west. The masts cut proudly through the night, a precisely fixed, softly resolute trajectory.

> I say to the night: go more slowly; for
> dawn will scatter the darkness.

December 9

I didn't get my sudden squall. I told myself: You'll see, it's always when you stay up till four in the morning, just when you most need rest, that it gets up and you have to go on deck.

But I didn't get up at eleven, either; far from it. I began and completed a magnificent dishwashing on deck, which gave me the chance to wash my hands and legs a bit at the same time—all because I wanted to make some pastry (I needed the pan and the salad bowl).

No meat or fish yesterday. I began to feel in urgent need of some. But it's all right now. While I was washing up a flying fish was cooking nicely and I've just treated myself to it before writing this. And now I'm getting down to the cakes: one third butter, one third flour, one third honey, and into the pan, in little mounds. I'll see what happens.

I still have too many links with the outside world: you should do this without books, radio, music, comforts. It would be a hard but thrilling experience, a retreat from the world.

The pastry's delicious! cooked very slowly and gently, on both sides, until it's crisp, as though it had been in an oven. . . .

Only another ten days, or less, if the wind holds up, because tomorrow I'll have done half the way in ten days. I've done 1,400 miles and there are 1,500 miles to do. Hurrah! With the marvelous winds I've had I could have beaten records if I'd had the right sails. But I'm sailing without a jib or storm jib and the mainsail is often flapping.

Today it's boiling hot. Not long now before I have a lovely cold shower on deck. Meanwhile I play some music, dance about like a madman, laugh, feel good all over. I've just eaten an avocado (they are delicious) and a tomato with mayonnaise. I've spent quite a bit of time working out calculations, averages, miles done, still to do, course to take, etc., forecasts. The beautiful Moroccan carpets, richly covered cushions, mirrors and particularly the large full-length one in the saloon, all give a luxurious feeling to my floating palace.

7:30. A good day. I've read a lot. I've devoured the *Express,* particularly the "If I Lie" columns by Françoise Giroud. I still distrust everything I read or hear, but you want to believe this newspaper when you discover that girl. Life at sea is conducive to exercising your intellectual faculties. You have to make a physical effort for twenty-four hours out of twenty-four, and end up by being alert all the time, and fresh, your mind clear, a bit like the Greeks, who studied while walking. I have an idea that women are bearing much of the burden in the evolution of our society. It seems to me that, liberated, they will cleanse the social climate, which has been made rotten by traditional male governments (men also becoming less and less so themselves).

Tenth day. Hurrah! I've had my bath: fabulous. Scrubbing brush, soap powder, buckets of sea water over my head, all on deck: absolutely gorgeous. What fun with it rolling like this. I've changed color—am a sort of scarlet. The sun's burning and the water's warm. I've found a very comfortable perch on the tackle that holds the two backstays from the mainmast, near the mizzenmast, and I stayed there listening to some music. Feeling on top of the world, I got down to make some adjustments to make us go faster: boomed out the jib to starboard, took the port runner and tackle for the mainmast right off because it's so far back that it stops the main

190

boom from going far enough forward when I'm sailing downwind. I can understand Moitessier when he went on to Tahiti. It's so marvelous, the best drug. On land to get the same degree of physical fitness you need a lot of will power to make the effort, to persevere. Very few people achieve it. Here one is passive, as if under artificial stimulants, but it isn't artificial, and so it's much better.

I'm at the "onlys" point now: (only eight more days!)

To think that in form like this and with a spinnaker I could do Cape Verde Islands–Barbados in a week: what a record. "SOLO ACROSS THE ATLANTIC IN 7 DAYS!"

As it is I've done two hundred miles for two days running now. There'll be a full moon when I arrive. I think about you and our two little girls a lot, and miss you all so much.

2 A.M. Impossible to sleep. I don't know how I manage not to be tired, sleeping so little. Problems with the jib tonight, rolling too much. Terrible desire to make love, too. "Don't wash, I'm coming!" Bonaparte wrote to Joséphine, during the Italian campaign. You can't imagine all the kisses I'm going to give you. If I had a spinnaker, I'd hoist it at once. Two, even! I'm so anxious to see you—relaxed, and happy. . . .

3 A.M. Qué pasa? Rain, veering wind, almost no wind. It was too good to last. All that talk of sails.

> Love has filled me with delicious torpors.
> Would that my keel would explode!

Oh how parched I am for love.

One week more at sea, if all goes well: no accidents, burns, fracture, food poisoning, falling overboard, squalls—dismasting—shipwreck or endless dead calms. I hope the contents of this letter will not be exclusively devoted to sex during this last week.

Goodnight, my love, my adorable, irreplaceable little wife. I would so love to be lying in your arms, to hold you and stroke you, to kiss you all over, all over, from the tip of each toe to your hair, taking in, on the way, armpits, legs, ears, neck, hair, tummy, buttocks, thighs, Achilles tendon, breasts, navel, mouth, eyes, nose, arms, hands, front, back, top, bottom.

An eternal night of love. Oh to go to sleep holding your

191

hand tonight, thinking only of you and of everything I will be able to give you tomorrow morning. I want us to make our next baby like that, wanting it, with all our strength, in the sun. So goodnight, my love . . .

Our minds are no longer on earth. We are like balls of fire, two complementary atoms, pressed together, drunk, crazy, in the universe. The surface of our bodies trembles and no longer belongs to us. We are one supernatural whole. Your poem which is always close to me gives me your answer.

> and you,
>   do you know?
>
> what
> this soft sweetness
>   is
>
> that floods
> my whole being
> to its
> depths
>
> what this
> exuberance is
> that explodes
> overflows
> compells me
>
> what this fountain is
> clear as ice
> sun leaping
> and why
> the sun
> becomes my friend
> the sea a dream
> around me
>
> why this air
> I breathe
> and all that touches
> but does not keep me
>
> why

192

all these
are so much part
of you?*

10:30, December 11

Good morning, love. I had hardly opened my eyes—I had already thought about the night I had just spent with you, and smiled to myself—before I had to go out and struggle with the jib (taken down in the night, broken sheet, fallen halyard). It's fixed now. I'm skimming along at eight knots toward Paradise, with 1,760 miles on the log. There'll be a lot of work to do when I arrive, but I've decided to leave it and rejoin you immediately.

Only another 1,000 miles, at midday. If I keep up the 200 miles a day I'll be there in five days, on the 16th—2,900 miles in sixteen days, which means an average of 187 miles a day. I don't dare think about it. Half the time we took with the *Alpha*. My course is perfectly straight on the chart. How I wish you were here. . . .

12:30. Rain! Luckily the wind's not deserting me; far from it. . . .

". . . And lead us not into temptation . . ." I thought I was succumbing . . . because of a very ripe avocado of which I ate half, creaming the other half over my body—which almost brought me there. . . .

Big scrub-up on deck with brush and buckets of water, in spite of the bad weather. All at a steady nine or ten knots: flying along. Read a lot again. Do you know Wilhelm Reich, a psychoanalyst contemporary with Freud? . . .

6 A.M., December 12

It will be dark for a few minutes yet. Suddenly there's an avalanche of water and the wind's roaring violently, incredibly violently. I'm taken by surprise and unable to act, it all happens so quickly. An infernal din. I look at the compass: on course. The speedometer: stuck at ten knots. I go out—we're flying. It's better: the wind's

*Poem by France Guillain.

193

violent but the rain has stopped; I'm soaked but it doesn't matter because the air is warm. The sun's just about to rise, and on that side the sky is blue, red, pink, violet—and on the other, terrifyingly black. It's frightening to be alone under this great canvas, but at the same time it's unbelievably exciting. . . .

10 A.M. A new squall hit me, with incredible violence. Impossible to lower the sails with the wind astern and too frightened to luff up into the wind with all this canvas, which would have flapped for an hour while I dealt with each sail. And as I watched the great boom of the mainsail simply broke, very slowly, under the terrific pressure of the wind in the 120 square feet of sale. I had to save the sail. I tried to jibe the mizzen during a short calm to take the wind out of the mainsail and lower it, but it was impossible. All this time the boat was yawing terribly and the jib cracking furiously, the boom threatening to break and pierce it with one of the splintered halves. I really had to fight, sweating in spite of the rain, sometimes hanging by one arm when a lurch took my footing from under me.

It was hard getting the jib down too, especially taking off the boom, which, with one end in the water, was bending desperately. So here I am with several hours' work ahead of me: carpentry, sewing, and painting, and still the same urgent desire, which I have no wish to "sublimate." Without the mainsail the boat's still doing nine, ten, eleven knots.

11 AM. Fascinating, on a reach now: it's safer with this violent wind. Still with no mainsail, the needle of the speedometer has just pointed to maximum, jammed on the zero, about fifteen knots. . . .

Beautiful night. Orion directly ahead of me, the Great Bear and the Pole Star to starboard and the Southern Cross to port. The Evening Star and Venus behind us. There's a fairly strong breeze and that consoles me a little. I don't mind breaking everything if I get there sooner. . . .

December 14

What torture this separation is. . . .

Four more days. I'm maintaining an average of 160 miles a day, still without mainsail, which isn't bad.

So I'll arrive on December 18 and I'll cable you at once. . . .

194

I'm going mad (no joking). I would never have imagined how challenging it is. I fight against it, tell myself that others have done it, that it's only fourteen days. . . .

You don't know how low I am. I force myself to eat a bit, to survive. Completely psychological my lack of appetite. I talk to myself in the mirror, or talk to the sea, think up reasons to go on hoping: it's crazy. I've still got plenty of vegetables and fresh fruit, but have opened my first can: cassoulet with two eggs. The last avocado. It's when your morale's low that accidents happen, illness, even death. . . .

Barometer very low. I'm jittery about these squalls that hit me with violent gusts several times a day.

Last page of the pad; I've no more paper.

> So, carried ever to new shores,
> Driven onward through eternal night,
> May we not anchor for a single day
> In the vast ocean of time?

15

Call of the Sea

Christian's solo voyage came to an end at last, at Barbados, eighteen days exactly after setting out. The best time done this year. Las Palmas–Barbados has become a real motorway, and it's more crowded every year.

But three-quarters of the navigators are newcomers to the game, made optimistic by listening to the accounts of their predecessors. They are still green on arrival—often with fear. The size of the waves, strength of the wind, accidents and breakages on board. True, they tend more and more to use standard boats with short keels, which yaw so much that it's impossible to trust the steering to an automatic pilot. The latter, moreover, breaks in the majority of cases, and they arrive exhausted from taking watches, and disillusioned. Only about a tenth want to go on to Panama. The others consider selling their boats. The more courageous sail theirs back to Spain. So, bravo, *Pygmalion.*

Now, for a while, we're dreaming wild dreams of our regatta thoroughbred in fiberglass, for our solo family voyage, of having the most beautiful hull possible. We walk in the countryside, near the little house where France lived with Laurence and Mareva, and talk and talk. The Pygmalion sold well; we must make another boat, but the question of fiberglass bothers us. Our dream racer, large enough to make comfortable cruises in—another boat of steel, a safe material which has proved its worth to us?

Or another "Joshua," the "Joshua" of our dreams—light, with aluminum masts, lead ballast, a flush hull. The low prices of the beautiful American fiberglass hulls tempt us—but so does a new "Joshua." For a month our wild enthusiasm seesaws from one to the other, and we can't decide. We know where we are with the "Joshua." It's heavy. Sailing on the wind, the most usual way for us navigators, the "Joshua" has the drawback of all ketches: the wind is taken out of the mainsail by the mizzen. On the other hand, as soon as there's any weather, even if you take down the mainsail, the mizzen is still too big. So you'd have to turn her into a yawl, that is give her a much smaller mast aft.

In the end the scales tipped in favor of the "Joshua," and in spite of the cost we decided to go for this. With great skill Yves Contandriopoulos, a young architect in Marseille, designed a very modern roof and cockpit, worthy of the finest racing yacht, and giving a huge flush deck.

While we waited for the hull and deck to be finished, we went to build up our strength in Espalmador, a beautiful little island in the Balearics, to conceive our third baby there, in the sun on the white sands. Afterward we went back to the shipyard, and a new adventure began: sandblasting, melting lead, painting, and so on. Two good months' work.

Those four months in Espalmador were a rest cure for us; it was a haven of well being and happiness. We conceived our third boat and our third child consciously, with all our hearts. With all our strength, now after ten years of uncertainty, quarrels, disappointed hopes, adventures gone wrong.

I need hardly say how impatient we were to see our floating

fortress, which we called *Le Tonnant,* in memory of a boat of that name that Aubert Dupetit-Thouars commanded at the battle of Aboukir. Aubert, one of Christian's ancestors, died gloriously, giving his last orders from a barrel filled with straw, because he had just lost both legs. His nephew Abel signed the act of cession of Tahiti to France with Queen Aïmata Pomaré.

I painted the large letters, identical to those on the warship, myself, in black on white.

Her builder gave us very generous terms. He wrote: "We want to thank Christian Guillain most sincerely because he gave those less well-off the assurance that one can still sail as our grandfathers did, on simple seafaring boats, but ones on which everything has been thought out and considered carefully."

She's the lightest "Joshua" there is. She is also, without any doubt, the most streamlined, with her hull and roof. Christian eliminated all unnecessary superstructures: you can bicycle on deck.

Le Tonnant, our pride. Nothing in the world would make us want any other boat. She is pure and beautiful. Born of our years of experience of the sea, and of our successful relationship as a couple. We are comfortable there: she's a home for us and our children, and we have taken advantage of the bigger area to give the children their own room, so that they have space to enjoy themselves. Enjoyment complemented by effort.

Twenty days ago *Le Tonnant* was skimming out to sea, all sails set, her canvas taut, sailing close to the wind with a fresh breeze. She is resting in a Spanish creek, champing with impatience to go to the isle of Espalmador. Our little Aïmata, princess of Espalmador, has been born.

"Well—South America? Or the Indian Ocean via the Suez Canal, opened especially for you?"

"With Laurence, Mareva, and Aïmata?"

"Of course!"

> "Would that I could gather your houses
> into my hand, and like a sower scatter them
> in forest and meadow."
>
> —*The Prophet*

198